RAILROADS

THEIR RISE AND FALL

A Personal Observation

By

Herbert E. Bixler

Published by

Herbert E. Bixler

Jaffrey Center, New Hampshire, 03454

ISBN 0-9610066-0-9

PRINTED IN THE UNITED STATES OF AMERICA

FOREWORD

Thanks are due to many, but especially to Agnes Bixler Kurtz for invaluable experienced consultation in the problems of publication and systems analysis, to Sidney Rodgers Bixler for wise counsel, to Elizabeth James Bixler for advice in grammatical questions, and most of all to Agnes Rodgers Bixler for rearing and nurturing all of the above while the author was putting in railroader's hours on the job and for inspiration and love.

TABLE OF CONTENTS

TABLE OF CONTENTS Continued

CHAPTER I

BEGINNINGS

The story of railroads needs to be told and understood for reasons far more profound than mere nostalgia or their fascination to a large body of devoted admirers. More basic is the study of what their development accomplished and how their decline came about. The simplistic notion that they were merely displaced by newer and better means of transport cannot stand against two observations: (1) wherever institutional barriers are even partly removed railroads serve well and prosper and (2) even under incredible institutional handicaps they provide, however ineptly, a service essential to the economy.

If we are to trace this story we must begin with a careful definition of what a railroad is. Railroads have been with us for so long and for most of that time have been so pervasive a part of our lives that they have many images. To some they represent the evil doings of bad old robber barons, to others the sweet nostalgia of comfortable travel to the accompaniment of the steam engine's whistle in the night, to others an obsolete dinosaur who refuses to lie down though headless, to others the triumphant magnificence of the steam locomotive's challenge to time and distance, to others political issues to enhance an office-seeker's glory - the list is endless, but none of the images serves the purpose of a definition on which to base a consideration of their rise and fall. Without such definition the origin of the railway or railroad* is as shrouded in mystery as the source of the Nile. If we mean any arrangement of rails on road to support and guide flanged wheels the origin is ancient and probably unrecorded. Certainly such works were in use in British coal mines and iron works long before the nineteenth century. Indeed, rutways, merely an inversion of the same idea, go back at least to Roman times, and the Romans built some in Britain with the ruts 4 feet 8 inches apart. This apparently was the standardized Roman pace, what we would call a double pace, plausible if the Romans' small stature is remembered. At least some of the early British tramways were built to this gauge, presumably to fit the wagons built for the Roman rutways. One of these was the Killingworth Tramway, for which George Stephenson built locomotives, and when he built the Stockton and Darlington, the first common carrier railroad, in 1825, he used this measurement plus 1/2 inch "to ease the fitting". Four feet 8 1/2 inches is standard gauge to this day, although many a battle was fought before it was settled.

But we haven't settled our definition. What makes a railroad significant in an economic and thus in a political and historic sense is the application of substantial power to the pulling of not one but a train of wagons whose flanged wheels are guided by the rails. This is the first repetitive or mass production, resulting in a quantum increase in productivity. To accomplish this significant advance the early tramway needed something much more powerful than a horse, and the opportunity appeared when James Watt invented the steam engine. Putting the young

*We choose to use the word *railroad* rather than *railway* only because we are concerned primarily with experience and development in the United States, where *railroad* heavily dominates popular usage.

monster on wheels and converting its reciprocating power to rotary motion, so easy and commonplace to us, was far from easy for the mechanical engineers of the day. It took 44 years, but Richard Trevithick did it, and in 1804 his locomotive hauled a train for the first time anywhere on the Pennydarran Tramroad at Merthyr Tydfil, about 20 miles north of Cardiff in Wales. This is the first instance which meets our definition. It was not a common carrier but carried only iron for the iron works on whose tramway it ran. It also didn't work very well, but the vital process of using high-pressure steam was established. It is interesting to note that contemporary efforts to operate a steam highway vehicle failed, largely because the roads couldn't support it. Even if the roads had been strong enough, however, the highway vehicle would not have produced the economic break-through which our definition remarks because without rails to guide the following wagons the essential mass production would not have been accomplished. The railroad, on the other hand, provided not only a feasible means of constructing a road capable of bearing a steam engine's weight, but guidance for the following wagons as well.

Trevithick's use of high-pressure steam, plus Blenkinsop's and Hedley's demonstration of the relation of weight to traction culminated in George Stephenson's invention of a successful locomotive. His *Locomotion Number 1* was built in 1825 for the Stockton and Darlington Railway, a common carrier hauling everybody and everybody's freight rather than just the property of its owner. It still stands on display at the Darlington station. No matter to which of the inventors you give the credit, the resulting ability at greatly reduced cost to transport over land a volume of passengers and freight previously associated only with shipping was a heady stimulus. At first, as might be expected, the new means of transport hauled only what had previously been hauled on highways or canals, but a free people was quick to take advantage of its superior capabilities. It was especially felicitous in North America, where continental distances and massive production of wealth awaited the means which the railroad provided. In the United States eager nationalism and a young nation's yen for development seized on the new means with the customary confrontation of the zeal of promoters versus the caution of the conservatives. In 1812 Col. John Stevens of Hoboken wrote a pamphlet extolling railroads over canals, pointing out that a locomotive could haul "suits" of carriages weighing 100 tons at four miles per hour. A commission of the New York legislature chaired by Gouverneur Morris proved conclusively that it was impossible, much as our federal government has asserted that two-hour travel between Boston and New York is impracticable. Oliver Evans, a brilliant inventor from Philadelphia, commented that 15 miles per hour, or 300 miles per day, would soon be practicable. He later predicted a New York - Washington journey by daylight, and even foresaw sleeping cars. Oliver Evans was ahead of his time and died unrecognized, while the country chose to develop canals. In 1825, the same year the Stockton and Darlington Railway was opened in England, the Erie Canal was opened in New York State. The canal was a great success from its opening until the predecessor roads to the New York Central Railroad were built, whereupon it became a ward of the state.

Nevertheless, Colonel Stevens and other enthusiasts persisted, and in 1827 construction began on the Baltimore and Ohio Railroad. Although the line had intended to use horses, the famous race between the early locomotive *Tom Thumb* and a horse convinced the management that it should become America's first steam railroad. Incidentally, the horse won because *Tom Thumb* suffered a mechanical failure, but the management saw beyond the incident to the future potential. Others followed quickly. The South Carolina

Railroad was chartered in 1828. The Philadelphia and Columbia, later the main line of the Pennsylvania Railroad, was begun in 1830. In the same year the Boston and Lowell, first of Boston's famous triplets, was chartered, followed in 1831 by the Boston and Worcester and the Boston and Providence. The normal resistance to a revolutionary idea receded quickly in the face of the economic and social success of the new enterprises. Both farmer and manufacturer welcomed the opportunity to get their products to a larger market at a much lower cost than by wagon or canal boat. People in general welcomed the opportunity to broaden their horizons by many magnitudes for either business or social travel.

Two basic decisions were made in this very early period which were to have determinative consequences. The first was to consider the new device not a public highway in different form, but a controlled private right-of-way, even though dedicated to the public use. There is no clear record of why this decision was made, but the assumption is that it resulted from the discovery, probably in horse-drawn days, that the inflexibility of flanged wheels on rails, the same technological change that permitted the quantum jump in productivity (and thus much lower cost) required more control over movements than highway travel. Probably the arguments between two opposing drivers as to who would back to a turnout waxed eloquent. Whatever the reason, the decision set the stage for one of those insoluble problems over a century later. When improved highways and motorized vehicles created an unprecedented competitor for the railroads the disparity between the different cost structures made it virtually impossible to regulate such competition, as we shall see later. The difference in cost structures is caused by the difference between owning the right-of-way on the one hand, a fixed cost, and on the other hand paying for the right-of-way as it is used, a variable cost.

The other decision was to grant a franchise to each new railroad, giving it both eminent domain and freedom from competition in a defined area. Presumably it was considered impossible to raise the huge amount of capital needed without this protection, but whether this was a justifiable fear is impossible to say in the absence of a test. Certainly intense competition did take place in the first half century in spite of it, but the far-reaching consequence was to give railroad management a sense of messiahship from which it never recovered. In the frantic competition of early days this made less difference, but when the protective mantle of regulation was thrown over them, railroads became very jealous of their turf and protective of real estate. This exclusivity of franchise and the common carrier concept which went with it were important in the development of regulation and in the resistance to deregulation, as we shall see.

Another feature of the early days which is much spoken of but seems far less important is that of government aid. Railroads' modern competitors, who owe their recent successes largely to uneven government policies, love to talk about this aid, but it was rarely if ever the kind of largesse recently granted air lines and waterways. It took two forms. Certain states granted real estate tax exemption, customarily for a strip of land five rods wide, enough for a four-track line but not for larger terminal properties. States and towns frequently bought stocks and bonds to help lines get started, but this was an investment, not a grant. The federal government's loan at 6% to the Union Pacific in fact put that line in bankruptcy, as we shall explain later. Some roads in the West received land grants, but it should be remembered that anyone who settled in the West received a land grant. The only thing different about the railroads was that they alone had to pay for their grants many times over by reduced rates on mail and government freight.

To return to the early successes, the result of eager public response was amazing growth. From 23 miles in 1830 the United States network grew a hundredfold by 1840 and well over a thousandfold by 1860. By that time the Northeast was fairly well covered, the South had skeleton service, and lines had begun to penetrate west of the Mississippi. This in spite of unprecedented capital requirements, beyond the capacity of the government in those days. The New York Stock Exchange in its earliest days listed only 12 stocks, eleven railroads and Western Union. Much has been written of the importance of railroads in the Civil War, especially the fact that a large army could be moved quickly and then supplied from the rear without having to live off the land.* Two political results were the Union Pacific and the military railroads of Europe.

*General Sherman said, "No army dependent on wagons can operate more than a hundred miles from its base because the teams going and coming consume the contents of their wagons."

CHAPTER II

IMPACT ON SOCIETY

The unprecedented demand for capital mentioned briefly in the preceding chapter was only one of the overwhelming impacts of the railroad on the society of the nineteenth century, but it was both fundamental and characteristic. Our society has so enormously expanded its capital investment that it is difficult to describe the impact of this first huge capital requirement in terms which are meaningful today. One way is to point out that our forefathers had never before seen or even read about any industrial or commercial (non-agricultural) undertaking which required such heavy investment, with the possible exception of a few banks. It is worth noting that at least in North America this need was beyond the capacity of the governments who (in a few instances only) undertook to supply it. One example which comes to mind is the Commonwealth of Pennsylvania's attempt to build a system of inclined planes over the Alleghenies, an undertaking which collapsed for lack of capital (and bureaucratic bungling) and was later developed into a railroad by the Pennsylvania Railroad Company. Another is the strenuous but abortive effort of the Dominion of Canada to build a transcontinental line, taken over and successfully completed by the Canadian Pacific Railway.

These are not pure examples of size of capital requirement, of course. Another variable is the political urge to do something for which there simply is no economic justification at the time. An interesting instance of this is the true story of the Union Pacific, the result of Fogel's able research told in his *The Union Pacific Railroad.* * We were all brought up to believe that the Union Pacific, our first transcontinental, was built as a result of the wisdom of the federal government in spite of shocking graft and corruption on the part of the entrepreneurs, acting under the name Credit Mobilier, graft which caused the early bankruptcy of the road. As Fogel points out, the fact was that the road was built at least ten years before it was justified. Because of this the equity, which the government insisted be provided by the private sector, was completely unobtainable except by the device of using the profit from construction contracts, a device roundly denounced by later journalistic historians who didn't bother to look up the facts. What bankrupted the company was the six percent first mortgage which the government imposed as security for its loan. Because the railroad was built before enough traffic could be developed, as investors had foreseen, the interest couldn't be paid and the road went bankrupt. In addition to correcting the myth the story contrasts the crushing mortgage laid on the railroad with the profligate largesse more recently lavished without recompense on other forms of transport.

There was of course much overbuilding for other reasons scattered throughout the network. For example, the early small railroads of New England were highly competitive (in spite of charters, whose restrictions they simply outgrew), and they sometimes encouraged the building of even lesser roads whose justification was questionable. The eagerness of communities thus "put on the map" to promote sale of securities made this all the easier. A geographical obsession of the day was the "Northwest Passage", a

*Robert William Fogel, *The Union Pacific Railroad,* Johns Hopkins Press, 1960.

somewhat vague concept that access to the riches of the West lay through a northwesterly approach to the Great Lakes. When the Fitchburg Railroad appeared to have an edge by association with the Cheshire Railroad across New Hampshire's southwest corner, the rival Boston and Lowell encouraged the building at great engineering difficulty of a roughly parallel line through mountainous country serving but one small village not otherwise served. This line (the so-called Keene Branch from Hancock to Keene, New Hampshire) was but one reasonably representative example of defensive action among many. It should be noted that, unlike the politically-inspired debacle of the Union Pacific, these maneuvers generally did not result in bankruptcy. The weak lines were absorbed into the nascent systems, to whose productivity they either contributed or not. If not, their losses were easily absorbed by the tremendous increase of productivity created by the industry as a whole.

This increase in productivity was the basic and greatest benefit conferred on the nineteenth century economy. Its source was simply the fundamental characteristic of the device outlined in our definition of a railroad - the ability to apply substantial power to the hauling of not one but many wagons, thus greatly reducing the effort required to haul each. Effort is reduced whether measured in energy consumption or human effort. A locomotive's fuel costs far less than a horse's feed (per ton hauled) and an engineer can move far more tons much faster than a teamster. This reduction in cost can be dramatically set forth by comparison with the apparently cheap transportation offered by native porters of a primitive culture. One such man, if very strong, might shoulder 200 pounds and carry it 20 miles in a day (to make sure we overstate the possibility). That's 4000 pound-miles, or two ton-miles. Even if he received no true wages, such a man would have to consume at least 50 cents' worth of food at today's prices just to stay alive. Ridiculously understated as this cost is, it amounts to 25 cents per ton-mile. Railroads pay union wages, support a fat bureaucracy, pay taxes, buy oil at today's prices, all from a gross of less than one tenth of that amount per ton-mile.

This quantum jump in productivity meant that agriculture could seek the most fertile fields even at a distance and supply people's needs at lower cost. Specialization, with its further cost reduction and quality improvement, could and did develop until the North American bread-basket became a staff of life to the whole world. Industry could seek its raw materials anywhere and spread its products far and wide. Consumers were no longer restricted to the products of local enterprise. So trivial became the cost of transport that Boston-made shoes could compete in the St. Louis market with those locally produced and St. Louis shoes could sell in Boston. Industry location was importantly changed. In colonial times Europeans skilled in copper and brass working settled in the Naugatuck Valley in Connecticut because there were copper mines there. They would have been forced to migrate to Montana or Chile when the mines gave out if it had not been for this revolution in transport. They haven't moved, but for a century or more the copper has been brought to them from far distant mines and the products of application of their skills to it go everywhere in the world. People hate to leave the area they have come to call home, as witness the miseries which coal miners will endure to remain in the hills where coal used to be mined.

Or for another example consider the skilled machine workers, used to working to fine tolerances, who settled in the area just east of Hartford. By the twentieth century these people were making airplane engines which were then moved (by rail) to the west coast to be put into airplanes and flown back east. Or the machine tool industry in that lovely valley in Vermont where Springfield is. Far from raw materials, far from markets, but a delightful place to live. So easy has the once back-breaking labor of transport become. And instead of queues of unemployed porters and horse drivers we have demand for new skills, enormous undreamed-of production of new wealth, much less poverty, and far more comfort, together with new challenges to man's ingenuity.

The specialization which went along with this new freedom of location also permitted the application of mass production techniques to manufacturing and agriculture, still further increasing the production of wealth and lowering of prices. This whole development made the nineteenth unique among centuries in that prices declined at a nearly steady rate (temporarily interrupted by the Civil War) for a total drop of some 25 percent. That we have not permitted this felicitous trend to continue in the twentieth century is due to our own folly.

Along with this explosion in freight transport went a similar and much more observable surge of passenger travel. This had economic consequences, too, because everybody could extend his business horizon, but it contributed far more than that. The cultural, political, and sociological results of vast horizons are as varied but obvious as they are difficult to describe. Political, religious, artistic leaders, would-be leaders, and educators could travel far and/or attract audiences from afar. Parochialism, the source of so much ignorance, superstition, fear, bigotry, and strife, is always diminished (even though never, alas, exterminated) by travel. The more travel is brought within the reach of many, the greater the diminution of these evils. We see today a further development of this principle as long-distance air travel is opened to millions. So it was when the countryman could easily go to the city, or the city-dweller to other cities.

No wonder our ancestors spoke of the iron bands which bound the nation together.

This major cultural change was observed by many a writer with no special ties to the new industry. Nathaniel Hawthorne wrote "Railroads…are positively the greatest blessing that the ages have wrought out for us…they spiritualize travel!" (*The House of the Seven Gables*) Thoreau referred to the railroad more than once. Emerson admired it.

All this enrichment of life would be enough to make the railroad the darling of the age, but there was more. The device clearly caught the imagination as much by its intricacy and functional beauty as by its accomplishment. Again there is nothing in present-day culture to which to liken its appeal. The airplane is thrilling, the auto is a mechanical marvel, space flight is breath-taking, but none of them has captured our fancy in anything like the way railroads dominated nineteenth century living. The reasons for this certainly include the fact that we are today so jaded by the rapid and accelerating pace of the appearance of new wonders that we have little capacity for wonder left.

Not so the public which welcomed the new marvel with admiration and joy. They had not only never seen anything like it, they had not seen anything at all which was in the same sense completely new rather than simply a modification of some familiar device. First in popular fancy, of course, was the locomotive. It breathed fire - it acted like a live thing - it performed prodigious feats of strength - the intricate motion of its pistons and connecting rods was fascinating - it moved like the wind - it even panted while resting. It was like a horse, but no horse was like that. Of course the name iron horse was affixed early and never lost. The development of the steam locomotive from Trevithick's and Stephenson's first efforts to, say, the Niagaras of the New York Central in the 1940s is a subject well worthy of a book in itself, and many good books have been written about it. Although there have been important changes such as the superheating of steam, the locomotive early assumed its basic form. The use of exhaust steam to improve the draft in the firebox, which gives it the distinctive chuff, identifies it and endears it to small boys of all ages. That sound, emitted so deliberately as the heavy train starts, then accelerated into a compelling rhythm of pride of achievement to which is added the defiant challenge of the whistle (in North America traditionally deep-throated) must move the most phlegmatic if he has a soul at all.

Then there was the track itself. Built to engineering standards far more exacting than any highway it ran now through deep cut, now at dizzying height, an artifact which was both beautiful to look at and exciting to travel over. Many writers attest to the joy of riding over it, above and beyond the satisfaction expected to result from arrival at destination. "Bless me this is pleasant, riding on the rail."

An aspect of the railroad which is not so obvious as the physical equipment is the system of control of operations whose development was forced by the constraints of the rail on the flanged wheel. Trains are guided, not steered, and cannot swerve to avoid an obstacle. Furthermore, unless held to very low speeds (certainly no more than 15 miles per hour) they cannot stop within the engineer's range of vision. This inherently extremely dangerous attribute produced a series of ingenious responses which had the effect of turning the new device into by far the safest form of transport ever devised. Since the train cannot swerve or stop, the trick is to keep the road clear for it. This was accomplished by a fairly intricate arrangement of rules, schedules, and procedures known in the trade as operating by time table and train order. The time table referred to is not the folder issued to the public to inform them when the trains could be expected, but a more complete set of schedules indicating when every train was scheduled to pass each station. This constituted an authority to proceed and a warning to all concerned that at that precise moment the track must not be occupied or otherwise obstructed. A logical system of rules worthy of today's computer expert evolved which accomplished the necessary orderly operation to ensure safety and unhampered movement.

It will be immediately apparent that such a system depends on a degree of precision in timekeeping which is rare enough today and was unheard of when railroads were developing. The new demand, as usual in a free society, evoked the supply, and another new industry was born to provide the railroad watch. Railroad workers, knowing their lives and the lives of others depended on it, made a fetish of the precise time. At every division point, that is at every local and regional headquarters, there was officially designated a standard clock, whose accuracy was checked by telegraph every noon with Naval Observatory time in Washington. If it was within five seconds the deviation was posted plainly alongside. In the rare event that it was more than five seconds off it was corrected. All railroad crews checked their watches with this clock when going on duty and thus were able to tell time to the second throughout their tour of duty. From this dire necessity developed a whole new standard of punctuality for a society previously pretty much content to tell time by the sun. The precision and dependability of passenger train operation which resulted from this necessity and from pride has never been equalled. Trains were sometimes late, but at least on heavily-traveled roads a late train was rare enough to form an acceptable excuse for missing an appointment. Certainly air lines, who handle most of the non-automobile passengers today, have no such standard of time precision, as any passenger with an accurate watch can observe.

The importance of time in operation led not only to punctuality but also to standardization. In early railroading days every town had its own time, probably somewhere near the sun's time at that point. At first railroads operated on the time of their headquarters city, but this made for great confusion to travelers changing from one railroad to another. Finally in the 1880s a convention of railroad passenger agents convened for the purpose established standard time, dividing the United States into four zones with time precisely one hour apart. (Canada extends so far east that it requires an additional zone.) Eastern time, which happens to approximate solar time in Philadelphia, was set just five hours earlier than Greenwich Mean Time, previously established as the standard for Great Britain. Before the railroad simplified, speeded, and stimulated travel it made very little difference whether local times varied, but with rapid and easy travel it was a tremendous convenience to have all parts of one zone keep the same time. Of course it also exacted a penalty in that the extreme eastern and western portions of the zones noticed the deviation from solar time. In the early twentieth century this fact caused Massachusetts, which, being well to the eastern side of the eastern time zone chafed at the early sunset, to establish by state law a summer differential. This had the effect of putting their state into the next time zone to the east, that is with Halifax, during the summer only. The confusion started all over again, exacerbated by the assumption of authority over time by the Interstate Commerce Commission, who ruled in the name of safety that railroads might not have anything to do with the new-fangled Daylight Saving Time, as it was called. After a generation of frustration the ICC ordered a regular pattern of shift each summer, with railroads and everyone else following the same time.

The time spacing of trains, as it is called, is completely safe, even in its primitive form, but it limits the capacity of the line. Very early in railroading a system of distance spacing, keeping trains a certain distance apart by some form of signal, was used. This developed into the automatic block signal, a beautifully simple fail-safe device which both increased capacity and kept trains apart even if human error disrupted the time table and train order system. The basis of its fail-safe nature is easily explained. A semaphore is so weighted that it will assume a stop (horizontal) position by gravity. It is held in clear position (usually upright but sometimes in the lower right quadrant) by an electromagnet, actuated by a current running through the two rails. When a train passes over the rails it shorts the circuit between them, the magnet loses its current, and the semaphore falls into stop position. Any failure of the current, caused for instance by a broken rail, sets the signal at stop. Instances of false clear indications are so extremely rare as to be considered non-existent. As signaling developed into more and more sophisticated electronic devices it continued to depend on modifications of this same basic scheme. Fail-safe mechanisms represent the most important characteristic differentiating train control from the control of highway and air vehicles, which still depend in the final analysis on human response.

In later years centralized traffic control, whereby dispatchers at headquarters can set signals and throw switches throughout an area of hundreds of miles, still further increased line capacity. Fail-safe electronic devices prevent erroneous operation. A still more recent device, automatic train control, stops a train at a stop signal even if the engineer fails to do so. Today's most sophisticated development is called automatic speed control, which means virtually automatic operation. If the engineer should become incapacitated the train would operate perfectly normally and safely.

In ultra-high-speed operation in other countries this is considered a necessity since action must be taken faster than can dependably be left to human response. All of these modern devices have replaced the primitive time separation, but the tradition of punctuality and precision of timekeeping remains.

It is not too much to say that the tradition of punctuality in the industry made several generations of people in all walks of life conscious of time and the benefits in both courtesy and practical accomplishment of respecting the minutes as well as the hours. People became aware of time's importance by learning that if they boarded their train even as little as ten seconds before departure they would make their appointments. If they attempted to board it ten seconds late it would be gone and they would not. Today we travel by auto or by plane and no such precision of timekeeping attends us. The exigencies of air travel require us to arrive at the airport far ahead of scheduled departure and any precise relation of actual to scheduled departure time is purely coincidental. Is it as a result of this that we have become so discourteously unpunctual in our comings and goings?

The orderliness and predictability of movements on a railroad brought about by both the channeling effect of the flanged wheel and the requirement for precise timing is in itself satisfying. Agatha Christie has her sleuth Hercule Poirot continually call for "order, method, and the little gray cells". Regardless of the state of our gray cells most of us favor an orderly march of events with matters turning out as they should. One very special reason for our approval is safety, and accordingly a system was developed out of procedures and devices based on and enhancing the intrinsic orderliness of rail technology. This system resulted in ability to move trains quickly through busy junctions and terminal approaches at headways measured in seconds, all under fail-safe protection which human error could not disrupt. The spatial requirements are also small, with the result that capacity to move passengers or freight exceeds that of other transport modes to a degree measured in orders of magnitude. Safety is far greater than that of the auto, whose driver can weave at will, or the airplane, without fail-safe signals and dependent on the human abilities of the controller and pilot.

On a larger scale the orderliness of movement required the development of a new skill quite apart from the civil and mechanical engineering skills which built the railroad. The scheduling of trains and distribution of equipment is easy if there is but one line from A to B. On an intricate pattern of lines in a developed country of many cities and towns, however, individual journeys may originate and terminate anywhere, and it is necessary to weave a pattern of schedules which at the optimum permit all connections to be made in minutes. The successful operation of an intricately interwoven pattern of course requires a very high degree of dependability. For this reason as well as to provide good service the maintenance of schedules became a matter of urgency among railroaders to a degree which stopped just short of obsession. If you can imagine a huge clockwork open to the elements you can begin to understand the effort required to maintain dependability in difficult weather. Any railroader expected to go without sleep for long periods at fairly frequent intervals. Train and engine crews were protected by a law forbidding their remaining on duty more than 16 hours (later reduced to 12), but in times of emergency others worked far longer. An emergency might be anything from a heavy snowstorm to a major derailment (railroaders considered the word "wreck" taboo). The motivation for the effort which made possible the very high degree of dependability which was achieved is not easy to define. Money may have been a large part of it in early times, because at first railroad pay was most attractive, the alternative usually being to work as a farm hand. Later there were many industries offering opportunities to make money, but the tradition had been established. Certainly pride, peer esteem, and the satisfaction of feeling esential had much to do with it. Railroaders habitually boasted of their long hours under difficult circumstances. That their remarks took the form of a lament may have fooled some, but not those who knew them best. The urge to display more stamina than the next man certainly contributed. Sometimes foolish and unnecessary privations were endured, but the net effect was that the trains ran mostly on time almost regardless of the weather, and the public came to expect it.

Human beings with a particular experience tend to associate with others who have shared that experience, an association which can sometimes become highly exclusive. The more fascinating and demanding the experience the greater the exclusivity. Railroad men and women, involved in a job which demanded the sacrifice of traditional daily patterns of work (no more homeward wending o'er the lea at dusk) formed a community of their own separated in many ways from the community at large. Fred Cottrell has analyzed this sociological phenomenon most skillfully in his excellent work *The Railroader.** One form of the exclusivity of railroaders which can be amusing is the jargon which developed to meet the need of brevity and clarity of understanding. Although there are regional variations, the language is perfectly understood by all English-speaking railroaders in North America. An example which will illustrate its color and its incomprehensibility to outsiders is the following account of an accident made by a trainman directly involved. It was a statement made to the superintendent investigating the accident which precisely describes the occurrence in detail,

*Fred Cottrell, *The Railroader*, Stanford University Press, 1940.

gives the location and activity of each crew member, and provides substantial evidence on which to base findings of responsibility. Here is his statement:

> We'd just pulled the drag off the main stem onto the two streaks of rust, but she hung over. I was up ahead bending the rails, the hoghead was on the ground greasing the pig, and the tallow-pot was up on the tank cracking diamonds. The con was in the doghouse flippin' his tissues and the rear shack was coolin' a red hub when he should 'a' been putting fifteen sticks between him and the drag, when the streak of varnish and plate glass came around the bend. The eagle eye seen us, threw her in the big hole, and give her two streams of sea-shore, but he'd been pounding her on the back, and they slid into us.*

For the movement of freight the intricacy of scheduling becomes greater than for passenger service and the problem more challenging, because the unit, in this case the car, cannot betake itself from one train to another as a

---

*Translation: Our heavy freight train had entered a passing siding but was too long to clear the main line. I went forward to throw the switch at the other end of the siding (to let my train out on the main line far enough to clear the other end of the siding), the engineer was walking around the engine lubricating bearings, and the fireman was in the tender breaking up coal. The conductor was in the caboose checking train orders and the flagman was dealing with a hotbox when he should have been proceeding fifteen telegraph poles to the rear (for flag protection), when the fast passenger train rounded the curve to our rear. The engineer saw us, applied brakes in emergency and sand to the rail, but he had been running at high speed, and the passenger train collided with our rear.

passenger can, but must be switched. Originally cars were simply moved one division (roughly 100 miles) and dumped helter-skelter onto the next division, but this cost time and money. Intricate plans are now made for advance classification to minimize repeated switching. The concentration of switching which results has led to the construction of huge classification yards over whose humps strings of cars are pushed for automatic switching by gravity under computer control.

Alas, the very intricacy of the pattern leads to a certain rigidity. When a schedule has been worked out in detail, the skilled person who accomplished it hates to see anyone tinker with it. This rigidity adds to the conservatism resulting from the sense of proprietorship caused by the franchise and heavy investment in real estate mentioned in Chapter 1. To this add the natural human feeling of pride in accomplishment on the part of those roads which were successful and it becomes easy to see why attempts to establish cartels were so persistent in the mid-nineteenth century. Those directly concerned with operations, including practitioners of all of the various skills required, went through the normal human cycle of eager innovator to proud achiever. Younger innovators would tend to balance their conservatism, but the industry needed such huge capital resources that it was dominated by financiers. The desire of the latter to see their investments protected tipped the balance which might otherwise have been achieved heavily in the direction of conservatism. In most of the many books and articles written in the late nineteenth and early twentieth centuries about railroad development "competition" is a dirty word. It was easy to advance the proposition that two railroads merely forced each to operate at less than optimum utilization of capacity. The repeated attempts to establish cartels failed, however, as all cartels do unless maintained by force, but the railroads discovered by chance that they could secretly support the populists of the day and thus obtain the force of government to maintain the desired cartel. Thus regulation was established, as we shall investigate more fully in the next chapter.

CHAPTER III

THE STULTIFYING EFFECTS OF PROTECTIVE REGULATION*

The widespread acceptance of the myth that railroad regulation since the last quarter of the nineteenth century has served to keep transportation costs down and protect the public from an ogre image of railroad monopolistic profiteering has acted to prevent the formation and pursuit of public policy systematically designed to promote the public interest and encourage the most effective allocation of resources. Such widespread acceptance as well as the falsity of the myth rival the persistence and error of the popular notion that Richard III was a hunchback who murdered the two princes in the tower in spite of its repeated exposure by historical researchers. The older myth at least had the strong raison d'etre of promulgation by no less a publicity agent than William Shakespeare, but our more recent myth has no such excuse for existence. Nevertheless our children are still taught that the Interstate Commerce Commision came into existence to protect the common man from the railroads, who were combining to prevent the forces of competition from lowering their rates. The truth is, however, something remarkably close to the diametric opposite. At least the major and most effective support of railroad regulation came from

*This chapter was published in 1968 as a monograph included in *Business Logistics*, edited by McConaughy and Clawson, by University of Southern California Press.

those railroads who desired governmental action to strength-
en and sanctify their own *unsuccessful* attempts to destroy
competition by agreement, or as they found it desirable to say
publicly, to "regulate themselves". Not only is the cause of
regulation different from what we have been taught, but the
effect has clearly been to keep rates up by stifling the
cost-reducing innovations which competition would have
fostered, as inter-modal competition is now fostering them,
although still partially hampered by regulation.

To understand the climate which nurtured the
Interstate Commerce Act it must be remembered that at the
time the railroads were far from new. Their development had
proceeded far beyond the stage of the fledgling air lines at the
time when the promotion and control of aviation became a
governmental concern. The railroads had developed for a half
century from perhaps the most astounding innovation of an
era famous for revolution and the emergence of new
thoughts. This innovation of the application of mechanical
power to the hauling of loads on a track which guided the
wheels of following wagons was successful to a degree rarely
if ever equaled. It did not merely move business executives in
a hurry to distant cities, it moved unheard of masses of people
and goods at speeds which at the outset were faster than
anything else and which rapidly increased, and, most important of all, it reduced costs of land transportation well below
that of the cheapest means then known, the canal. It was this
last attribute which made it so successful in a sociological as
well as a pecuniary sense. It permitted food to be moved from
where it could easily be grown to where there were masses of
people who would otherwise starve. It permitted fuel to be
moved from where it is found to where it is needed. It
permitted manufacturing to be so concentrated as to permit
tremendous increases in efficiency and the most effective
application of skills while yet distributing the results far and
wide. Thus it opened continents to man's adventure and

permitted the flowering of man's inventiveness. With such an excess of economic contribution over cost, it would be surprising if the railroads had not prospered. They grew rich. Just as naturally they reached the point in their existence which in the development of a civilization is called by Toynbee its time of troubles. As happens to individuals, the industry, or at least a substantial part of it, had reached the point where it wearied of its strenuous youth and sought to protect and pamper its corpulence.

The political climate which led to the enactment of the Interstate Commerce Act has been shown by Professor Kolko, in his clear and thorough analysis of the available data,* to be quite different from the myth of the chaining of the railroad dragon. From his examination of the letters and testimony it becomes apparent that strong support for the concept of regulation came from railroad managements who had tried for some time to enforce rate agreements. He points out the rapid decline in freight revenue per ton-mile during the closing decades of the nineteenth century. He goes on to record the lack of success of attempts to control competition by rate pools. "Numerous pools were organized throughout the period - there were at least eight in operation in 1879 alone - but with only one exception they all rapidly failed."**
He goes on to describe the famous Iowa pool, that initiated by William H. Vanderbilt of the NYC in the East, and various others in other regions, characterizing the results of the

*Gabriel Kolko, *Railroads and Regulation* 1877-1916 (Princeton, N.J.: Princeton University Press, 1965), p. 22.

**_Ibid._, p. 8, with reference to U.S. Treasury Department, Report on the Internal Commerce of the U.S., 12/1/1879 (Washington, 1879), pp. 164-183.

first-named as "a most uneasy alliance with constant infractions…". He concludes his listing of the various attempts with this sentence: "Given the failure of voluntary pools to create some semblance of reason and stability in the railroad system, despite successive attempts too numerous to itemize here, railroad men then turned to the government for possible regulation."*

In view of the important influence of economies of scale on the cost characteristics of a railroad, it seems beyond doubt that the railroad managers of the last century sought large volume from large shippers by offering rates which in a crude way reflected such cost characteristics. This was bound to be looked upon as discrimination by those shippers who did not have sufficient volume to command the lower rates, without regard to, or even knowledge of, the cost effects on the movement of their own freight.

This cry of discrimination was clearly a cry for protection just like the demand for a protective tariff. Competitive railroads seeking large volumes of additional traffic by offering low rates to large shippers did not thereby increase the costs nor the price of their existing traffic. They may have lowered them. The shippers who sought protection by legal action preventing such cost and price reductions were acting from the same security urge as the railroads who sought protection from their more aggressive fellows. The impulse to seek authority to suppress the development of an innovation which threatens to supplant one's established procedure is natural, ancient, and widespread, but to succumb to it inevitably destroys economic advancement.

*Ibid., pp 10-11.

Professor Kolko points out that the oil producers
first introduced the legislation which was the forerunner of
the Interstate Commerce Act, not because they were
anti-railroad, but rather because they were anti-Standard
Oil.*

Kolko later points out the support of railroad
leaders to such legislation, based on their inability to enforce
their pooling agreements. He quotes several such leaders as
supporting governmental control, and even an apportionment
of traffic.**

That the incidence of fixed costs in a railroad's
capital-intensive economic structure necessarily results in
destructive competition between individual railroad companies has been frequently cited as the justification for railroad
regulation. Certainly stability was more to be desired than
competition. Competition meant rate cutting, and rate cutting
meant discrimination. In any case, the Interstate Commerce
Act which resulted from the political forces then in existence
was almost obsessed by a horror of discrimination. The whole
of Section 2 is devoted to its denunciation. At a much later
date, however, when other modes came under regulation, no
special attention was given to discrimination. The promi-
nence of Section 2 in Part I of the Interstate Commerce Act
(which covers railroad regulation) is contrasted with the
absence of any similar provisions from the other parts of the
Act, which cover other modes, in an earlier article:

Section 2 of Part I is unique in its
isolation. In its only paragraph it prohibits discrimi-

*_Ibid._, p. 22.

**_Ibid._, pp. 26-27.

nation, which it defines as charging one person more or less than another for a "like and contemporaneous service". No similar section appears in the other parts. Since Section 3, which forbids undue or unreasonable preference or advantage, covers the same subject and covers it more fully, there is no reasonable explanation for Section 2 except as an angry reaction to a practice that inflicted some injury, either fancied or real. Considering the effect of what economists call economies of scale on railroads, that is, that large volumes can be handled at lower unit cost than small, it seems likely that railroads offered rebates to shippers of large tonnage in recognition of this economic fact. Doubtless small shippers, jealous of the practice, found it easy to arouse politicians' oratory, the more so since railroads were always a popular political whipping boy and politicians notoriously care little for economics.*

Competition destroys value-of-service rate making, which the early canals favored,** the early railroads imitated, and the voluntary railroad pools attempted to enforce. Its benefits were, however, so generally favored that it was not politic openly to denounce it. Excerpts from the Commission's first two annual reports testify to their adoption of value (note that value-of-service has now been simplified to value) as a basis of rates:

*H. E. Bixler, "A Psychoanalytical View of the Interstate Commerce Act," *Traffic World*, September 4, 1965.

**Kent T. Healy, *The Economics of Transportation in America* (New York: The Ronald Press Co., 1940), p. 201.

The public interest is best served when the rates are so apportioned as to encourage the largest practicable exchange of products between different sections of our country and with foreign countries; and this can only be done by making value an important consideration, and by placing upon the higher classes of freight some share of the burden that on a relatively equal apportionment, if service alone were considered, would fall upon those of less value. With this method of arranging tariffs little fault is found, and perhaps none at all by persons who consider the subject from the standpoint of public interest.*

The business of a railroad company as a carrier of freight is to exchange for the people the products of different sections and countries, and this exchange, as to many commodities in a country so large as ours, or indeed in any considerable country, would be restricted to comparatively small sections if articles which are at once bulky and cheap and articles which in small compass comprise very great value were alike charged rates for transportation which disregarded the value as an element of estimation.**

This attempt to prevent discrimination while encouraging competition posed a difficult dilemma for the regulators. Confusion as to meaning and precise definition only made matters worse, as is explained in a recent report to the Department of Commerce on cost-based freight rates:

*Interstate Commerce Commision, *Annual Report,* 1887.

**Interstate Commerce Commission, *Annual Report,* 1888.

Almost two centuries ago, when the most modern forms of transportation were the turnpike and the canal, it was first recognized that a transport service which could not be self-supporting on the basis of one price to all users or units of use could be self-supporting if different users were charged different prices, or if quantity discounts or special rates based on time differences were offered to the same user. This practice of price differentiation (a) was justified on the ground that one price to all would either produce revenues inadequate to maintain the service, or choke off some demanders who might, if served at lower rates, yield at least some profit which could in turn be used to lower the highest prices charged.

(a) Usually called price discrimination, it refers to the existence of differential ratios between prices and costs, and therefore cannot be assumed to exist when the question at issue is precisely the relationship of rates to costs.

As for price discrimination, compare G. Lloyd Wilson: "... discriminating pricing is practiced by charging different prices for goods or services produced and sold under conditions in which the differences in the prices are not attributable to commensurate differences in costs of production or distribution," "Inherent Advantages - Summary and Conclusions," in *Essays on Inherent Advantages of Railway Service*, New York, Simmons-Boardman Publishing Corporation, 1954, p. 44.*

*Systems Analysis and Research Corporation, *Cost-Based Freight Rates-Desirability and Feasibility,* Prepared for the Under Secretary for Transportation U. S. Department of Commerce, Cambridge, Mass., August, 1955, p. 51.

The establishment of regulation had the effect of enforcing conformity and protecting the producer of transportation both from the pressures of competition and the importunations of shippers. A rigid and extremely complex rate structure began to take shape, any change in which was looked upon as harmful to the national interest. By a very simple process of reasoning the interest of the railroad system was identified with the national interest. Since the maintenance of a strong transportation system of common carriage was essential to the national welfare, then it followed that what was good for the railroads was good for the country. It all seemed good at the time and even now we are only beginning to see that the effect of regulation was to protect the transportation industry from the birth-pangs of creative innovation. Even as late as the 1930s it was clear to an individual beginning to learn the railroad business that it was easy to fall into the habit of meeting customer requests and complaints by making reference to regulatory law, thus brushing the problem under the rug rather than attempting to cope with it.

At the time it was not apparent that any innovations were needed. The cost of moving coal was heavily influenced by the high unit costs associated with low utilization of the cars involved, but even in the unlikely event that penetrating cost analysis brought this fact to light, why should anything be done about it? Certainly there was no incentive to a railroad to reduce its rates so long as they were protected by regulation. If the unit train concept were advocated it would very easily have been shot down. It would destroy the rate structure, thus placing the national transportation system in peril. Furthermore, it would be clearly discriminatory, since most users were not big enough to receive a train load of coal at one time. Of especial significance, the *pro forma* costs would be based on something new, that is, a degree of car utilization never before achieved. This the regulatory body would never accept, preferring to trust to the more comfortable and conservative figures borne out by experience. The ICC took exactly this view in the famous Big John case in 1963.*

This innovation is almost purely a change in procedure, requiring no technological break-through. It is inconceivable that it should not have occurred to many involved in the daily task of transporting coal, and its implementation requires only planning and systematizing, without the need of any new or untried tools. Nevertheless it was effectively suppressed, not only by the utter lack of any incentive, but even by the protective paternalism of regulation. The innovation did come about and the economy now enjoys the efficiencies which result from its widespread use, but it could only come to light when competition beyond the reach of protective regulation forced action.

Similarly for many years new automobiles were transported in specially designed box cars, four autos to a car. Only when 93 percent of the business of transporting new autos had been taken from the railroads by highway haulers did the auto rack car come into existence. The auto rack car is not a technological break-through any more than the unit train. It is merely an application of the idea that loading more autos on a large open car will materially reduce costs.

Other examples could be named. Anyone who worked for a railroad during the era of peace and tranquility has had the experience of seeing old ideas, stultified by the

*Grain in Multiple Car Shipments-River Crossings to the South, 321 ICC 582(1963).

bureaucratic attitude at that time of management, labor, and regulator alike, come belatedly into being under today's more competitive climate.

The tragedy is not the delay to a few ideas since developed, it is the suppression of who knows how many and what nature of unborn innovations. We like to remind ourselves that we live in an age of marvels undreamed of a short time ago. What should concern us is the equally undreamed-of marvels that might have been. In the days of their early development, uninhibited railroads developed the technology of passenger transportation to the point where 100 miles per hour was demonstrated and accomplished. If such development had continued, instead of being stifled by the bureaucratic assumption that the market had been saturated, is it not possible that we might now find it unnecessary to resurrect a moribund technology?

The first indication that the protective structure of regulation might not be impregnable was the appearance of a new means of motive power for the most ancient of all modes, highway transport. During and soon after World War I it became apparent that certain transport jobs could be done better by the motor truck than by the railroad. The cost of the motor truck might be greater or less than rail cost, but it was very difficult to tell. The rate structure, deliberately related to value and carefully protected by regulation, bore no relation to cost whatever. Trucks could offer rates for commodities of high value which were below the established rail rates without regard to whether they were below rail costs or not. The rigid value-based rate structure in theory took the revenue necessary for the maintenance of a transportation system from those commodities which could most readily afford it, to the benefit of other commodities, lower in value, but necessary, which according to the concept of value-based rates would not have to bear their share.

Obviously in order to make such a system work it was necessary to require that the less lucrative tasks be performed. This was accomplished by the designers of regulation by reaching back into the middle ages for the term "common carrier" and applying it to this need. The previously hotly competitive railroads were given this title and required to serve all comers at published rates, a requirement rigidly enforced by the full majesty of the law. This atavistic application of mercantilist concepts and expressions was convenient in other ways. It permitted the enforcement of a requirement that all places be served as well as that all commodities be carried. The small shipper in a remote village had the same standing as the steel mill in the metropolis. This was a very peaceful concept, but of course as easy a prey to the selective competition of the new and unregulated trucks as the outposts of the Roman Empire to the Huns. High-rated commodities could be attracted by rates somewhat less but still far from cost, and shippers advantageously located could be served without regard to those in remote places.

The effect of this new competition was not that which might be expected from normal competition in a free market place. At least two generations of railroad men had been brought up in the climate created by regulation to believe that their services were essential *in toto* and that their rate structure was sacred. That they had certain economic strength in certain areas is now apparent from the success of recent innovations, but their habitual reliance on the protection of regulation prevented the channeling of their resources into the most productive application, as might be expected to happen in a free market place economy. They did not meet the competition by basing their pricing upon their cost advantages for certain types of haul,* but sought to recoup

*Ernest W. Williams, Jr. *The Regulation of Rail-Motor Rate Competition* (New York: Harper and Bros., 1957), pp. 221-222.

lost revenue by general rate increases, thus increasing their vulnerability.

They also sought to extend their protective coverage by bringing the new competitor under regulation. This seemed to offer a peaceful solution to the problem, and the ICC's authority was extended to motor carriers and those other newly-troublesome competitors, the inland waterways. There are some fundamental differences in the kind of regulation imposed on the different modes,* but the greatest problem arose from the entirely different cost characteristics of the different modes.

Parenthetically, an early attempt to apply the principles of a protected rate structure to the new problem is found in an ICC decision handed down in 1937. Here it was suggested that rates be made higher, not on commodities of high value, but on non-competitive traffic.**

It gradually became clear that the ICC could not relate the rates to the costs of the competing modes under

*H. E. Bixler, *op. cit.*

**"Faced as to some traffic by the competition of other forms of transportation which are able and willing to quote lower rates, the railroads have the alternatives of losing such traffic or of keeping it at rates which pay less than a *pro rata* share of expenses and return. In such circumstances, the only way to maintain a satisfactory financial condition is to charge the traffic which is not subject to competition more than its *pro rata* share of expenses and return. Such procedure, also, is not unfair to the noncompetitive traffic, so long as the resulting rates are not greater than they would be if the competitive traffic were not handled, and so long as the maximum possible revenue is obtained from the latter traffic." Source: Interstate Commerce Commission General Commodity Rate Increases, 1937. Ex Parte No. 115, 223 ICC 657 (pp. 738-739).

their juristiction; could not, in the words of the national transportation policy, develop the "inherent advantages" of the different modes, because the completely different cost characteristics of those modes made them impossible to compare with each other directly. The study of cost-based freight rates previously referred to illustrates by reference to a long series of cases the dilemma which the ICC faced as a result of this cost problem.* The difficulty was that each mode would claim to be the low cost mode. For example, a railroad would propose a low rate based on its marginal cost for handling the traffic under consideration, but the competing mode would counter with a study showing that its full cost was less than that of the railroad. The cases cited show that the ICC was torn first one way and then the other. It quite understandably desired to offer the public the benefit of the lower rate, but equally understandably wished to protect the "low cost" carrier. Why should the low cost carrier need protection? Because the cost characteristics of the different modes are so dissimilar that they seem to produce contradictory analyses. The high incidence of capital costs in a railroad cost structure, and the relatively large capacity of most of its cost components, make the difference between its marginal cost and full cost sometimes very great. Because a motor carrier, on the other hand, pays for its right-of-way by means of fully variable user charges, and because its cost components are readily divisible into relatively small capacities, its marginal cost typically comes much closer to its full cost.

Even this highly simplified analysis leaves the regulator with no standard for relating rates to cost in such a way as to preserve the inherent advantages of the various carriers. Adherence to the full cost theory is inhibited by the

*Systems Analysis and Research Corporation, *op. cit.*

clear advantage of the lower rate offered. Adherence to marginal cost rate making is inhibited by a fear that it may in the future become higher, either by arbitrary action or by the economic effect of reaching full capacity, and that the competitor with the lower full cost will by that time have disappeared. The problem is capable of resolution, however, as we shall presently see.

In the meantime it should be noted that railroads are not the only transportation mode which has felt the stultifying effects of regulation. Professor J.C. Nelson's analysis of the effects of entry control on the motor carrier industry shows that in that mode also, the effect of regulation has been higher costs and larger companies in a dominating position.* The existence of large areas of motor carriage outside of regulation, notably haulers of products of agriculture, provides a comparison to the regulated industry. Dr. Nelson points out that the unregulated portion of the industry is characterized by low rates, small companies in intense competition, and strong opposition to regulation on the part of shippers.

The stultifying effects of protective regulation have left us virtually unable to cope with the "problem" of price reductions which follow technical or procedural innovations. The interesting thing is that price reductions should be thought of as a problem. In the transportation field we are so inured to the protection of the producer that it makes us uncomfortable when a producer passes on a cost reduction to the consumer. This is a strange attitude for government, certainly inconsistent with the concept of the regulator as the protector of the public. It leads to a concern

*J.C.Nelson, "The Effects of Entry Control in Surface Transport," *Transportation Economics* (New York:Columbia University Press, 1965).

that regulation in other fields might have the same result of turning the desired objective upside down.

In the transportation field it leads to a very specific concern regarding the policy of minimum rate regulation. It is now clear that even if it were desirable to return to the practice of complete rate regulation on a value of service concept, it is no longer possible, because of the large segment of the transportation industry which is unregulated. To remove rate regulation all at once would undoubtedly produce chaos, at least temporarily, because it would take time for an industry so long accustomed to the protection of regulation to adjust to the rigors of the market place. A gradual transition can, however, be begun without delay.

The key to resolution of the dilemma seems to lie in the fact that the fear of a marginal cost basis of rates is unfounded. The failure of a proposed rate to bear its full share of all costs is not harmful. That portion of the costs not being borne by it are already being borne by something else and they are not increased by the application of the new rate. In fact, to whatever extent the new rate does exceed marginal cost, they are lessened. That marginal cost should jump because capacity is reached is of course theoretically possible, but it is most unlikely. The railroads, who champion marginal cost rate making (now that competition has sharpened their ingenuity) suffer from chronic underutilization and are not likely to reach capacity in the foreseeable future. If it should happen, however, the salvation lies in the prompt availability and fiercely competitive nature of the trucking industry, particularly that portion of it which is not subject to regulation.

It remains to determine how much above marginal cost a rate may be. It seems clear that the only non-artificial determination of this is to allow it to be shaped by demand. Averaging is purely artificial. Demand, however, permits an automatic value-of-service component with a substantial difference from the traditional rate structure. In this case the upper limit is sharply limited by competition. Thus value of service, demand, cost, and competition can automatically shape freight rates in such a way as to tend toward optimum allocation of resources.

This is, in fact, substantially the formula which the ICC follows when it decides a case involving competition from an unregulated carrier. All that would appear to be necessary to achieve the desired result is to follow the same formula in all minimum rate regulation. This would seem to resolve the current dilemma of minimum rate regulation, characterized in the previously quoted cost-based freight rates study as follows:

>...complicated by the different cost characteristics of the different modes, distorted by the traditional concept of the rate structure based on valueof-service pricing, obscured by the different impact of public costs, and thwarted by the very substantial area of unregulated transportation.*

The important lesson to be learned from this experience is that the stultifying effects of regulation, self-perpetuating for so long a period, were only attacked by the appearance of competition from without the protected area, beyond the reach of regulators. First the railroads were protected, and to a very large degree cost-reducing innovation was stifled. Then the competitive modes were brought under the umbrella of regulation. This created near chaos

*Systems Analysis and Research Corporation, *op. cit.*, p. 3.

within the fortified camp, with the apparently insoluble problem caused by conflicting types of cost structure, but attempts to solve it were all of the protective type. Only as a result of the pressure of unregulated competition, which arose fortuitously, have we been forced to allow a measure of freedom which has brought to light innovations long buried. Hopefully this measure of freedom will grow in transportation regulation and the lesson will be applied to our thinking in other areas where we are tempted to escape reality by a retreat into protective regulation.

*   *   *   *   *

Note added to later edition: Since the foregoing was published the Staggers Act of 1981 has substantially reduced railroad regulation, in effect following the thrust of the recommendation made here. As indicated above, adjustment will take time, but already (1982) there are signs of considerable improvement in the railroads' ability to react positively to market requirements and allocate their resources so as to optimize benefits to themselves and the economy.

CHAPTER IV

PASSENGER SERVICE

The earliest passenger car was a stage coach on flanged wheels. Soon it was three coach bodies on one set of wheels, leading to the compartmental arrangement which became standard in Europe. In that densely populated continent, where stations usually served cities or towns of some size, the method of operation has always centered on the station master, who collected the revenue and released the train for departure. In America, however, it became expedient to put the train in charge of a crew master called a conductor, who gave the signal to proceed and went through the train en route collecting revenue.

There is a story which is worth retelling in spite of its probably apocryphal nature. It is said that in the earliest days it had not been established whether the conductor or engineer (never in America called an engine driver) was superior in rank. A certain conductor rigged a rope along his train with a stick of wood at the end in the locomotive cab in such a way that when he tugged on the rope the engineer could see the wood move. He instructed the engineer to stop at the next station when he wiggled the wood, but in the event the engineer, who considered himself superior in all things, certainly in matters of train operation, ignored the order. When the train did stop the irate conductor challenged the engineer, and finding him unrepentant and obstinate, engaged him in hand-to-hand combat and vanquished him. Thus was the superior rank of conductor established for all time.

In any case, the American passenger car soon assumed the form of a single long room, entered at either end from a platform. Since American roads, like the country they served, were much less developed, stations did not have platforms at car-floor height, and so the car had steps on each side at each end. These were made feasible because the American car was so constructed that its strongest member was its centersill, and thus the side sills could be cut with impunity. The European car is built on strong side sills which cannot be cut without weakening the car. Thus when necessary in Europe to use steps for entering they are very steep ladders.

Every account of early railroad travel mentions snakeheads. This disastrous occurrence resulted from the use in very early times of strap rail, a strip of iron laid on top of a wooden beam. It was possible for the strap to become dislodged in such a way that the end passed over instead of under a car wheel, with the result that it was forced into the car's interior, with catastrophic results which can be imagined. Very early in their development railroads substituted solid rails, first of iron, and in the 1880s of steel, which of course put an end to the problem. To be sure, every disaster is of supreme importance to its victims, but most of those which stopped occurring over a century ago are forgotten. Undoubtedly the frequency of the mention of snakeheads is due more to their unique and dramatic quality than to any long-range importance.

The cars were lighted first by oil lamps, then by gas, both of which were dangerous in wrecks, of which there were many in the early days while the science and art of railroading were being developed. Electric lighting appeared about the turn of the century, the current being supplied by a generator belted to the car axle. Storage batteries kept the lights on when the car was standing, but if they ran low the lights would dim until the train resumed motion. Heat was provided by a stove, also a source of danger, until the practice of using steam from the locomotive was developed, sometime after the Civil War. The stove meant, of course, that the passengers near it roasted while those far away froze. Steam heat usually meant overheating because that was the only way to be sure no one and no pipes froze until the more sophisticated means of control of the twentieth century.

An enormous improvement came toward the close of the nineteenth century when closed vestibules at the ends of the cars permitted walking through the entire train in safety and comfort. Even before the Civil War, and to a greater extent afterward, some trains were introduced which were equipped with every luxury. The early transcontinental trains had private bedrooms, lounges, organs, baths, and were stocked with the finest of food and drink. Many books and motion pictures have made this so well known that it needs no further description here.

The first trains ran about 12-15 miles per hour, and New York State, with the customary solemn omniscience of government, passed a law limiting speed to 15 miles per hour, since it was well established that any higher speed would drive men crazy. Either they had faith in the greater fortitude of women or they didn't care. Speed increased fairly rapidly. One of the very earliest locomotives, named the Antelope, ran from Boston to Lawrence, 26 miles, in 26 minutes on a test run. After the Civil War enough experience had been acquired to make 60 miles per hour not unusual, and in the 1890s the Empire State Express of the New York Central achieved 112 miles per hour as a special effort. Unfortunately by this time the cartel made possible by regulation smothered the incentive to further speed increase, and this mark was not approached for 40 years. Parenthetically, every advance in speed has brought forth dire scientific proofs that any further increase would cause disastrous failure of something. The wheels would explode, we were told, or fall off, or the rails would break, or some other mechanical limit would be reached. The recent (1981) achievement of 236 miles per hour by a French National Railways train with no damage whatever to the train or track has laid to rest all such doomsaying up to that speed, at least.

The tragic effects of the stultification of railroad management by regulation were not instantaneous. During the early twentieth century considerable development took place in spite of the gradual increase of regulation. The effect of regulation can be seen in the fact that the development was internal and strengthening of the existing infrastructure rather than external and entrepreneurial. Passenger service, for example, continued to be improved in several ways even though in general speed was not greatly imcreased until the blossoming of the streamliners in the late '30s. There were exceptions, most notable being the appearance in 1899 of the Twentieth Century Limited over the New York Central between New York and Chicago with a schedule of 18 hours for the 960 miles. It was immediately matched by the Pennsylvania Special of the Pennsylvania Railroad, later renamed the Broadway Limited. Incidentally, that name has nothing to do with the New York avenue associated with show biz, but comes from the name given to the very substantial and highly engineered four-track Broad Way over the Allegheny Mountains between Harrisburg and Pittsburg, the salient characteristic of which is the famous Horseshoe Curve. Even these enterprising ideas, however, were immediately scotched by the prevailing ultra-conservatism engendered by the climate of regulation. Within two years their schedules were lengthened to 20 hours and remained at that level for a third of a century. These were lavishly-equipped trains, including observation cars and supplied with shower baths, barbers, and secretaries.

More important and more general was development involving multiple track, strengthening of bridges, improvements in signaling, and larger, heavier, and better-designed locomotives and cars. This had little effect on maximum speed but greatly improved safety, reliability, and comfort, minimizing delays caused by train interference or mechanical failure. With the development of the Pullman Company a standardized sleeping car service became available almost everywhere. For example, it would be difficult to name a city or town, even a fairly small town, in the developed region of New England, New York State, and Pennsylvania, which did not have a sleeping car service to New York City. Of course there was similar service in other parts of the country.

The standard 12-section drawing room car (with 12 lower berths, 12 upper berths, and a drawing room for the occasional opulent traveler) was not a palace, but it was remarkably comfortable and provided a means of getting over considerable distances without loss of working time. The gentlemen's dressing room doubled as a smoking room, with a comfortable leather couch which served as the porter's bed during his brief off-duty time. The latest and funniest stories were circulated in this room. The miracle achieved by the Pullman Company was that wherever one boarded, even far in the hinterlands, the car was always equipped with clean white sheets, clean towels, ice water, and the usual household offices, all under the care of a highly skilled porter. The local train through Newport and Claremont, New Hampshire, for instance, consisting of a small American type engine and two wooden superstructure coaches, dragged a huge Pullman, bound for New York. The Pullman Company entertained more overnight guests than all the hotels put together, and boasted that any one of their berths was the safest place in the world to sleep, not excluding one's own bed.

It should be brought out that one reason for the excellence of the service was the blatant race discrimination of the culture. Barred from most good jobs, blacks sought jobs as Pullman porters and dining car crewmen. These were the best jobs open to blacks, and the men who filled them were of much higher calibre than would have been found in such jobs in a free society.

Sleeping car service was so ubiquitous as to be found even between cities close together. So many people found it more convenient than going to a hotel that a whole train of sleeping cars ran each way every night between New York and Philadelphia, a 90-minute run. The cars were open at origin from ten o'clock, moved soon after midnight, and kept open at destination until seven, plenty of time for a night's sleep. Sleeping car service was remarkably inexpensive. Having paid the same railroad fare as in a coach, the passenger paid the Pullman Company only three dollars for a lower berth for some 200 miles, and only about twice that for 1000. After World War I the railroads required a surcharge of 50 percent of the Pullman charge. The Pullmans of the first third of the century were heavy (about 80 tons) and therefore responded to variations in the track level only sluggishly through heavy springs. This made for a most comfortable ride, and the boast of early automobile salesmen was that their products rode like a Pullman.

The design of the sleeping car and its use illustrates the difficulty which a regulated industry faces in coping with marketing problems. The standard Pullman seat, like the coach seat, holds two persons. At night the seats are lengthened by using the space of the opposite seat, thus conceptually providing a double bed. The upper berth, suspended from the ceiling, provided sleeping room for the occupants of the opposite seat, and thus the sleeper theoretically provides the same capacity as a coach, and the railroad is commercially justified in charging the same fare. The Pullman Company made its own separate charge to comsensate for the extra service, greater luxury, and provision of the car itself. The trouble was that passengers wanted private individual beds and the practice of selling one berth to two persons died early. This made no difference to the Pullman Company, whose berth charge was small in relation to the rail fare anyway, and who had no difficulty collecting this charge from single passengers, but the railroad in effect lost half the revenue with no diminution of cost. Then as sophistication increased passengers shunned upper berths unless there were no lowers available, and the effective capacity of a standard car dropped further. To increase the fare as compensation for this increase in both demand and cost, however, was unthinkable in the face of regulation. Railroads were rich, their freight service was lucrative, and passengers easily cried for protection from their rapacity. Conversely, efforts to develop a possible lower price market by lowering fares would be shunned for fear the lower fares would become standard by regulatory pressure. Thus begins the doubt of passenger service's profit potential and the cross-subsidy of passenger service by freight service.

The typical coach of the early twentieth century developed into a heavy all-steel standardized car with parallel rows of green plush seats. These seats were designed to have the backs flipped over at the end of the run (for some reason Americans, unlike the rest of the world, developed a phobia of riding backwards) and for long wear rather than comfort. Safety and economy were far more important to the regulated decision makers than comfort and beauty. There was no decoration, but there was a baggage rack overhead on which you could sling your bag if you were strong enough, and the car was lighted and heated - usually over-heated. The toilets were usually dirty. One amenity was always present - ice water and paper cups in which to drink it. The fare was

3 cents per mile before World War I and 3.6 cents thereafter, until the reductions of the '30s.

Parlor cars, usually but not always operated by the Pullman Company, provided premium fare service on day trains. They were equipped with comfortable swivel chairs, one each side of the aisle, carpets, and clean toilets. The gents' wash room was a smoking room, as in sleeping cars. Each car was in charge of a porter. Dining cars were mostly a joy. Plastic food hadn't been invented then, and everything was cooked on board, a somewhat miraculous accomplishment in those tiny kitchens. Fresh-baked corn muffins for breakfast were so delicious as to constitute sufficient reason to make the trip. Crisp starched linen, china and real silver gave an air of real luxury, and on crack trains each table would have a fresh rose. The worst problem of the diner was that on a crowded train it was necessary to wait in line to get in. Lounge cars, usually placed next to the diner at the end next to the Pullmans, served several purposes. Their comfortable upholstered chairs, usually placed facing across the aisle, provided a more desirable place to await room in the diner than standing alongside the diner's kitchen, the usual lot of the coach passengers. They also provided a place to buy a drink without crowding the diner (the porter served you at your seat) and a place where women as well as men could smoke. Especially they provided a place to which a Pullman passenger could repair at any time as a relief from the tedium of sitting in one place. The provision of lounge cars represented the greatest improvement in American over European travel. In Europe, where the big cities are much closer together and travel times therefore shorter, even first class passengers are expected to sit quietly in their seats except for a trip to the restaurant car.

This passenger service had more or less settled into a standard form until the '30s. The automobile had begun to cut sharply into the passenger business early in the '20s, but the regulated industry couldn't see what to do about it. The normal reaction of a regulated industry to lower volume is to ask for higher prices to make up revenue, but in this case it was apparent that such a move would only aggravate the problem. In the '30s the Smoot-Hawley Depression greatly increased the loss of traffic, and some halting steps to combat it were taken. For example, the New Haven bought coaches of a radical new design with comfortable seats, pleasing decoration, and, wonder of wonders, a smoking lounge in each car, with ash trays, yet. This lounge, open to view, and from which one could see his bag on the rack above his regular seat, pretty much solved the smoking problem. Fares were drastically cut, and for the first time a distinction was made between the two classes. Since the beginning it had been considered un-American to have second or third class fares, as in Europe, and the same fare (3 cents per mile before the war, 3.6 cents after) applied to all, except that the Pullman passenger paid the Pullman charges in addition. This meant that the Pullman passenger had to have two tickets, a requirement very confusing to European visitors. In the '30s a differential was established, the first class fare being 3 cents per mile, plus Pullman charge, and the coach fare 2 cents. Note that calling the lower fare second class was still taboo.

Probably the greatest improvement of all was air conditioning. This had been tried out by the Baltimore and Ohio between New York and Washington early in the decade and was very well received, as any one who has been in those parts in summer can imagine. It not only provided relief from the stifling heat, it meant that for the first time passengers could stay clean. Steam locomotives burned soft coal, and their cinder-laden exhaust streamed back over the speeding train. The cinders, tiny, hard, and black, infiltrated everything, especially when windows were open. Pullman cars were equipped with fine-mesh screens, but even so one's clean white sheets were covered with a black dust by morning. It was hard and could be brushed off, but it was undeniably a nuisance. Now at last it was possible to shut it out and enjoy the ride in clean as well as cool comfort. Air conditioning spread rapidly, and soon all Pullman cars, diners, and coaches on trains moving over 100 miles were air conditioned. It is of passing interest that throughout the '30s almost the only places where one found air conditioning were passenger trains and movie theatres.

After several decades of little change, passenger trains in the '30s began to be spruced up. The western roads, more entrepreneurial than eastern (and with a tiny portion of their revenue and cost related to passenger service), early installed reclining seats in coaches, and eastern roads followed. A real effort was made to keep coaches clean and to make their interiors attractive. Diesel locomotives were beginning to supplant steam, and both kinds were stream-lined. This idea, made popular by the development of the airplane, gave an impression of modernity and stylishness whether or not it was effective in increasing speed. Speeds were increased, however. The Burlington Zephyr, a newly designed diesel train, ran from Denver to Chicago, 1034 miles, in 15 hours, 38 minutes. The Boston and Maine and Maine Central operated a duplicate train, called the Flying Yankee, between Boston and Bangor. The running times of the Century and Broadway were cut not only to their original 18 hours, but to 16. The eastbound Century, in an effort to minimize the adverse effect of the time change, ran in 15 1/2 hours. The Pennsylvania Railroad electrified the line from New York to Washington and Philadelphia to Harrisburg. The Congressional Limited ran from New York to Washington in three hours, 35 minutes. The New Haven ran three trains each way between New York and Boston in four hours. The Superchief ran from Chicago to Los Angeles in two nights and one day, saving a day on the transcontinental journey. This was probably the most luxurious of all the posh transcontinental trains, with a dining room under a glass roof on the upper level of a bi-level car, a sunken nightclub beneath, and all the usual features. The California Zephyr, between Chicago and San Francisco, made good use of the newly invented vistadomes for passengers the better to see the magnificent scenery through which it operated. The vistadome was invented by a General Motors official who was riding in the cupola of a caboose when he was struck by the ability to see the mountains and thought it should be available to passengers. He devised a sort of glass bubble on the top of a passenger car, with seats on each side of the aisle from which one could see forward, back, to each side, and straight up. It was immensely popular and until the demise of passenger service operated on several western trains. Eastern railroads could not use it because it made the car too high to get into either New York City station, but the Baltimore and Ohio put one on the Capitol Limited between Washington and Chicago. None of the faster running times listed above is spectacular in comparison with air schedules, but current Amtrak schedules are for the most part much slower.

The Pullman Company radically changed the standard Pullman sleeper. Gone were the open sections, with upper and lower berths, replaced by private rooms. Innovative design produced a room small enough to be placed on either side of the center aisle but fully equipped for a night's lodging. Somewhat miraculously it contained a bed big enough for anyone but a basketball player, a toilet, wash basin, clothes closet, medicine chest, and luggage bin. The bed folded up into the wall to reveal a comfortable seat. After some revisions in the design based on experience the standard settled down to ten roomettes, as the small rooms were called, and six double bedrooms. The latter were also redesigned in ways which resulted in better utilization of available room, making them appear more spacious and livable. The partition between two bedrooms could be folded out of the way, and the result was an accommodation far more luxurious than the familiar drawing room of the former standard car. There were variations of the car's layout, such as 22-roomette or 11-bedroom, but the "ten and six" was the standard. With this new design a passenger could retire when he wished to a private room behind a bolted door or seek companionship in the lounge car when he preferred.

The new passenger locomotives which appeared in the '30s, just before the steam locomotive's demise, were of interest more to railroad men and rail fans than the general public, but they were magnificent. Three certainly merit special mention. The New York Central's Hudson type, a large 4-6-4, was as beautiful as it was powerful and fast, and it handled that road's impressive parade of passenger trains with ease bordering on contempt and with satisfying aplomb. The New Haven's I-5 had the same wheel arrangement and had unusually clean lines, giving it almost a streamlined appearance. Its superb capability made the four-hour schedule possible but it could have run much faster if the New Haven (whose curves added up to some 16 complete circles in 224 miles) had been straighter. The Pennsylvania's GG-1, the electric locomotive designed for New York - Washington service, has justly won the admiration of all locomotive buffs for its tremendous power, high-speed capability, the clean lines of its Loewy design, and its instant and continuous availability.

The diesel locomotive made its appearance just before World War II (there were small diesel switchers before that) and swept the country soon after, eliminating steam engines within a few years. Because of the notoriety of trains such as the Burlington Zephyr the media and the public got the erroneous impression that the diesel was a high speed engine, but as is so often the case, the truth is just about the opposite - its virtues are especially apparent at low speed. An illustration of the comparative performance of steam and diesel was afforded passengers on the Century and Broadway during the transition era. The Pennsylvania, partly because it had so successful a steam engine as its famous K-4s, had been reluctant to try to match the New York Central's larger Hudsons until about the time diesels appeared. They therefore were quicker to apply diesels, and for perhaps a year or two after the war the Broadway had diesel power while Hudsons still hauled the Century. The two rival limiteds left Englewood (where each made a suburban stop at the same station) at the same time and operated on parallel tracks for a considerable distance, a challenge to a race which the crews never ignored. When the disparate locomotive types were operated the outcome was foreordained. The diesel, having the advantage of its electric drive's continuous torque, accelerated much faster at low speeds, and the Broadway pulled away rapidly. The steam engine was typically clumsy and slow to get started, but when the Hudson reached about 35 miles per hour its high-speed characteristics became apparent, and its rate of acceleration increased dramatically. The diesel, whose engine had nothing more to offer, accelerated relatively sluggishly at high speeds. As a result the Century, with the Broadway now well ahead of it, overhauled its rival and swept majestically by, leaving a gap the diesel could not close. The diesel's appeal was not speed, but economy. Unlike the steam engine it did not require the attention after each run of an army of workers to perform dirty and expensive service, but was immediately available for the next run.

The story of passenger service would be incomplete without mention of the Railway Mail Service. Mail was carried on passenger trains from the first year they operated, and from 1838 until after World War II almost all of it was carried by rail. Although the postal service had in the horse-drawn days charged different rates for carrying letters different distances, movement by rail so reduced the transport cost that it was calculated at a small fraction of a cent. For that reason a uniform rate was set at three cents. Soon it was reduced to two cents, where it remained for decades until raised again to three cents in the twentieth century, the rate still prevailing at the time of World War II. The rapid climb to its present dizzying heights is recent, having occurred since the mail was taken off the rails.

In 1838 a railway post office car (RPO) was put in service in England, but its counterpart didn't appear in America for twenty years. This vehicle provided room for the sorting of mail en route and a catcher for picking up mail sacks without stopping. There was also a slot in the side of the car in which anyone could deposit a letter at a station where the train did stop. If one wrote a letter in the evening he could take a pre-bedtime stroll to the station and mail it in the RPO car. Of course the clerks could also toss sacks off as stations were passed, and the result of all these activities was amazing improvement in mail service. Most RPO's operated at night, and since the mail arrived at destination sorted and ready for delivery, overnight service was assured to almost anywhere within five or six hundred miles. By special arrangement overnight service could be extended. In Grand Central Terminal, New York, for instance, there was a mail slot designated for the Twentieth Century Limited. Letters dropped here up to a few minutes before departure (6:00 pm at the time of the fastest schedule) would be in Chicago, sorted for substations, at 9:00 am. This was too late for regular delivery, but a special delivery stamp, which cost ten cents extra, would ensure delivery that morning.

When the airplane and the truck took over the handling of first class mail it was decided that RPO's were too expensive and they were taken out of service. The assumption was that the speed of air transport would make up the time, but as all of us can now testify, no speed of movement seems to match the time saving of sorting en route.

Passenger trains also carried a sort of priority freight called express. Early in the railroad era an enterprising gent went around Boston soliciting parcels for delivery in New York, rode the night train to the latter city, and delivered them. From this grew the Adams Express Company, and many others sprang up in those vigorous days. This merchandise was carried in a baggage car, accompanied by an "express messenger", who, like railway mail clerks, carried a gun, to the fascination of small boys watching every move. The early express companies were merged into a few, became subject to regulation, ever more bureaucratic, and finally were taken over by the railroads' collective action and named the Railway Express Agency. Even though this agency operated as a sort of special air freight forwarder during the early airline days, it was unable to stand up to the competition of motor trucks and died soon after World War II.

During World War II government restrictions on gasoline use and absorption of most airplane capacity forced many people onto trains and brought passenger travel from the severe trough of its depression decline to record heights. The three large passenger roads, the New Haven, Pennsylvania, and New York Central, were inundated. Every piece of equipment that could run was pressed into service, some of it old and uncomfortable. It was not nearly enough, and trains were crowded with standing passengers to the limits of safety. The misery was made worse by air conditioning failures in summer and heating failures in winter, maintenance being thwarted by wartime scarcity of men and supplies and by the intensity of use. Unfortunately, many young people, brought up in the automobile age, got their first taste of railroad travel at this time, and were appalled. The cost characteristics of passenger carrying are such that over-crowded trains are very profitable, and the three roads made some money as a result, but at the price of almost the complete loss of their reputation for comfort and dependability.

After the war, therefore, these three roads decided to use the money earned by the war-induced traffic for a huge investment in passenger equipment. As a result most of their trains were made up of superb new cars hauled by diesels or electric locomotives on schedules as fast as had ever been run. This meant that the New York business man*, for example, could at the close of business walk or take a short taxi ride to Grand Central or Penn Station and catch an overnight train for Chicago, Atlanta, or any nearer city. On board he* would enjoy a dining car service matching most restaurants and a constantly available choice between complete privacy and pleasant club surroundings. His* arrival put him downtown with a good breakfast inside (except where arrival was so early that there was plenty of time for break-fast) at or before the opening of the business day. Thus no business time was lost. Nevertheless, by the late '50s virtually all of that traffic had deserted the trains for the air. It should be remembered that air travel in those pre-jet days was considerably slower and even less comfortable and convenient than it later became. Fares were higher than rail. But the typical businessman left his office in early or midafter-noon for the difficult and expensive trip to LaGuardia for a bumpy ride eating plastic food to take another long taxi ride to check in at a hotel late in the evening. Why? No really satisfactory answer suggests itself, but perhaps the prestige

*The use of the suffix "man" and pronouns "he" and "his" denotes common gender.

of letting it be known that one traveled by air was enough. In any case, the marketplace spoke very clearly. The railroads, having been isolated from the marketplace for three generations, had difficulty answering. Railroad enthusiasts inspired politicians to urge regulatory commissions to prevent the loss of any train. The trains ran empty, not only at great expense, but also causing deterioration of morale and service. To be connected with a once proud service which is obviously no longer needed is hard to take, and few employees could avoid surliness.

On shorter hauls the experience was much the same. Between New York and Boston in the late '40s trains were sumptuously equipped with new coaches, parlor cars, diners, and lounge cars. Trains left each end every hour on the hour, three of them making the run in four hours. They carried over three million passengers a year between the two cities, more than the total air, bus, and rail passengers 25 years later. Where the passengers went is apparent from a look at a column of annual volume figures. After the expected drop immediately following the war, the numbers held up reasonably well until the highway improvements reached the point that it became possible to drive the distance in about the same or less time than the train took, whereupon they plummeted.

Some efforts to fight back were made, largely inspired by the supply trade, always more entrepreneurial than railroad managers. Goodrich Murphy of the Budd Company invented a car which ingeniously fitted private rooms for 40 persons (eight of them in double rooms) into a standard-size car. This was offered on a few trains as an inexpensive sleeping accommodation for coach passengers, at coach fare plus a small room charge. It was well received.

The demise of rail passenger service was hastened by the deplorable lack of expertise in cost accounting and market analysis. Under regulation the railroads had long before settled down to a fixed rate per passenger mile, regardless of cost and demand. Decisions to provide or not to provide passenger service were based on political rather than economic factors. The cost of railroad service varies widely with the extent of its use. That is, it costs little more to haul a crowded coach than one which is empty, and by no means proportionately more to haul ten cars than two. Manning requirements, based both on union demands and on technology whose improvement was inhibited by such demands, set a minimum below which cost could not be reduced. Thus it is apparent that the country local, consisting of two cars, one coach and one combination baggage-smoker, carrying a handful of passengers, costs far more than its revenue. Furthermore, the country local was the first to lose its passengers to the automobile, whose convenience was a greater advantage to rural folk than to the user of the frequent service of inter-city expresses.

Any attempt to remove such trains, however, ran into the stone wall of politically controlled state public utilities commissions. These had for generations refused to allow trains to be discontinued on the theory that the railroad, a protected monopoly earning big profits from its business in general, must provide losing service in particular situations "in the public interest", a concept easier to declaim than to define. Faulty as this concept is at any time, it becomes outrageous in the face of (a) financial stringency of the railroads and (b) the obvious preference of the public for a new mode. The politicians stood fast. They protected the people from the rapacious railroads. They protected the crews from the greedy capitalists. That the people didn't ride on the trains and that the crews were well protected by seniority rights had no political significance. There is even one case where the railroad offered to provide a taxi for the three or four remaining passengers but was refused.

The experience of fighting this irrational opposition made passenger service a dirty word to railroad management. Managers were rewarded for their ability to reduce train miles. The lack of good cost analysis made management unable to distinguish between profitable and unprofitable segments of the passenger business. The whole showed up as a deficit in the somewhat clumsy accounting of the day, and it therefore slowly assumed the visage of an ogre. Slowly, because pride and habit made railroad managers reluctant to do away with the glamorous part of their business, but surely financial stringency forced a realistic approach.

Lack of marketing ability meant that it was not necessarily always realistic. Such lack affected decisions in two ways. Managers would attempt to use a through train to substitute for a local they wished to discontinue by adding stops to the through train, thus reducing its attractiveness to the through passenger and increasing its cost by adding to its consist. More important, with rare exceptions there was a lack of ability to analyze a market's potential to see how service could be tailored to demand.

Thus the drop in passenger business, gradual in the '20s, increased by the Smoot-Hawley Depression, interrupted by World War II, became precipitous in the '50s. The reasons customarily cited are either not true or not complete. It is in no way true that the railroads deserted the passenger. As detailed above, the decline dropped fastest and farthest during the excellent service immediately after the war. It is customary to say that the unions were intransigent and management stupid, but this begs the question. The protective regulation over two or three generations had given labor a monopoly and dulled or eliminated management's entrepreneurial sense. Because state utilities commissions foolishly resisted removal of trains carrying virtually no passengers management dared not experiment for fear any new train would have to run forever whether or not it was successful. Because of lack of marketing ability management had trouble devising such experiments, anyway. Government's huge largesse to other means of transportation considerably exacerbated the problem. In the '50s the drop left stations and trains virtually deserted, with the result that the former became hangouts for society's misfits and the latter lost all glamour and self respect. Then in the '60s the railroads in the Northeast, the principal passenger carriers, fell on hard times, the freight business could no longer support the passenger deficit, and track maintenance began to slip. This completed the collapse by reducing speed and spoiling comfort.

After several years of huge losses in passenger service, amounting to many millions of dollars extracted from railroads as surely as if it were a special tax, the government permitted the roads to buy their way out by providing the initial capitalization of Amtrak. The more they had lost, the more they were required to contribute, a type of justice worthy of medieval Byzantium. Unfortunately, the heavy passenger carriers of the Northeast, least able to pay because of their severe freight problems, were assessed the most.

Amtrak's service is almost universally slower than the post-World War II service, but it has a lot of new equipment bought by the taxpayers. Thus it is trying over again the experiment which the railroads tried right after the war, when lots of new equipment was put in service in a vain attempt to stem the loss. Meanwhile Amtrak cannot seem to provide the kind of advanced rail service offered in other countries, notably Japan and France. They promise us, for example, three hour 40 minute service between New York and Boston after well over a billion dollars is spent. Such a schedule, only 20 minutes faster than that of the '40s, cannot attract the passengers needed to make it viable. A careful and exhaustive study a decade ago showed that two hours 20 minutes, somewhat slower than speeds actually achieved in other countries, could be accomplished and would attract the necessary volume, but interagency feuds seem to make it impossible under the government's banner. In a later chapter we'll muse on what might have been.

CHAPTER V

FREIGHT SERVICE

At first the early railroads accepted freight at their various stations and loaded it on cars which resembled wagons for movement to a center city or a port. The primary purpose of many of the early railroads was to make access to a port available to interior cities, towns, and farms. Before the railroad era the principal transportation arteries were sea lanes, and inland areas were served only by wagons, whose expense prohibited the movement of anything but merchandise of high value. For example, it was possible in the early nineteenth century to grow grain west of the Alleghenies in great profusion, but it could not move to the seaboard, where the people who needed it were, unless it was first made into whiskey. In Europe the problem was met to a degree by extensive construction of canals to supplement and connect the natural waterways, and in America some canals were dug. By the time America was developed to the point of canal digging, however, it was only a few years before the appearance of the railroad. Because railroads were so much cheaper (remember the quantum leap in productivity produced by the flanged wheel), and to a lesser degree because railroads were faster and operated year round, the early canals, with very few exceptions, were soon abandoned. The most notable exception is the New York State Barge Canal, which continues in existence only because its costs are paid by the taxpayers of New York State. That the beneficiaries of this largesse are for the most part the large and prosperous firms who ship on it makes this bureaucratic distortion of the marketplace the more ironic.

The railroads, then, permitted the farmer and the inland manufacturer to send their produce to a port and thus to the world. As one might expect, the demand for this service mushroomed. Soon freight cars, as they grew larger, settled into four standard types. The common box car, a closed shed on wheels, was much more widely used on this continent than in Europe, both because of weather and to discourage pilferage. The open top car, usually with low sides, long known as a gondola, became the standard for material too heavy or bulky to load in a box car and not requiring weather protection. The flat car, merely a platform on wheels, carried such commodities as lumber or machinery which it was inconvenient to lift over the side. The hopper car came into general use primarily for coal because its high sides held a greater volume and the hoppers in its bottom permitted gravity discharge into bins below the track. As production increased under the impetus of cheap transport it became expedient to ship in carload lots, and this unit became a widely accepted commercial measure. Smaller lots, now called LCL (for less than carload) continued to be accepted at the stations and loaded by the railroad's agent.

At the same time the railroads were expanding and linking together to form a ubiquitous network. The pattern of commerce shifted, and the primary job became the linking of the seaboard with the interior of the continent rather than the ports with the hinterland some fifty or a hundred miles inland. At the same time the tiny railroads were merging into larger systems, still small by today's measure. The Boston and Maine, for instance, a small railroad among today's giants, was made up of over a hundred tiny lines. The systems created by these early consolidations responded to the shifting commercial demand and interchanged freight to permit shipment to all parts of the country. Each railroad supplied cars to its own shippers, and the lading had to be transferred at each point of interchange with another carrier. The cost and delay resulting from this labor-intensive requirement can readily be imagined. The first response was the establishment of private car lines, called fast freight lines, enterprises formed to supply cars which could run through on different railroad lines without transfer. This worked well for larger shippers who sent substantial volume regularly to the same destinations, but could not satisfy others.

As the nineteenth century progressed, the railroads succeeded in working out arrangements for the interchange of freight cars, and the problem was solved. Not without intensive effort, however. It was necessary to standardize many features of the freight car. The battle of the gauges was finally resolved, and the four feet eight and a half inches chosen by Stephenson as a modification of the Roman pace (cf. Chapter I) prevailed. Much more than gauge had to be standardized, however. The car had to be of a size which wouldn't hit structures alongside the track, and standard clearance diagrams, meticulously measuring width at each inch of height above rail, were agreed to. Rules had to be established to govern procedure if delivery of a car exceeding standard dimensions was attempted. Couplers had to be of the same height and of compatible type. Center sills had to be strong enough to take certain stress. These and similar structural requirements were established by mechanical officers, who also established detailed rules for governing the maintenance of another road's cars and the charges for same. "Owners' defects" and "users' defects" were carefully defined.

A new problem arose from the practice of free interchange of freight cars. It remained the custom for the railroad on which the shipment originated to supply the car, but now the car might be expected to go far from "home" (as the limits of its owner's lines came to be known) perhaps having traversed several different railroads en route. How was it to get home? The solution involved the establishment of a set of standards called car service rules and a new cadre of railroad officials known individually by various titles but categorically as car service officers. The rules they established required that each railroad accept an empty car moving over its home route, that is, the reverse of its loaded movement, and move it to its owner's rails at no charge. It will be immediately apparent that this requires massive record keeping. The waybill, the paper accompanying each loaded car and serving as the authority and guidance for its movement, was stamped at each interchange point and an interchange report made to the car service officer of the delivering and receiving roads. The former notified the owner as a means of discharging his responsibility. Of course each road kept records of movements on its line. The agent at destination reviewed the junction stamps on the waybill and made out a "home route card" which served as the authority for its return. All this paperwork, in the office and in the field, was carried on by hand, with ingenious devices for simplifying work, long before the appearance of office machinery. Railroads were early customers of the makers of such devices and now make very extensive use of computers. These car service officers were in constant touch with their counterparts on nearby roads and therefore developed a perspective somewhat more regional in scope than that of operating officials.

Beyond the region, however, warfare raged. The movement of freight from west to east is much heavier than vice versa. Raw materials have generally come from the west to the east. The process of manufacturing always reduces volume, and a large part of the product is consumed by the greater population of the East. By long established custom the western railroads supplied their own cars to their own shippers, and the cars became empty in large numbers in the East. As a result the eastern roads normally had a glut of empty cars and rarely suffered a car shortage. The car service rules permitted the loading of a "foreign" car (belonging to another road) only in the direction of the owning road, but violations of this rule were very easy to make. A shipper with a number of box cars just made empty at his loading dock might not be meticulous in the selection of those he loaded. A harassed agent or yardmaster might fill an order for a car with the first one available in order to avoid the considerable switching necessary to insure strict compliance with car service rules. In any case, the western roads, perpetually surprised at the fact that the loaded movement of their cars off line resulted in their not all being on line, jealous of the eastern lines' freedom from the car shortages from which they themselves periodically suffered , assumed the worst and accused the eastern lines of every sort of malfeasance and misfeasance. The battle raged for decades in the Association of American Railroads, before the Interstate Commerce Commission, and in the Senate, whose members from western states took up the cudgels for their constituent lines with a vengeance. In a free market, of course, the price system would have taken care of this sort of difficulty automatically, and nobody but a few specialists would know anything about it, but the regulated railroads settled most matters politically, unlike their forebears.

The argument centered around the payment made by a road for the use of another's cars. For a short time after interchange was opened up this was set as a mileage payment, but in order to add an incentive for prompt return a per diem (daily) charge of 25 cents was added. Soon the mileage charge was dropped and the per diem rate increased by steps to one dollar, where it remained for several decades. This charge was supposed to cover the cost of ownership of the car and no more, but the cost is difficult to establish with certainty. Repair costs are buried in the payments for all the things done by mechanical forces, and the value of cars varies greatly, involving different investment costs. These difficulties permit of heavy argument about the appropriate rate, settled by vote of the association. Because the vote was apportioned to the number of cars owned, and because eastern roads needed less cars by virtue of the difference in volume of freight by direction of movement, the western roads dominated. Eastern roads claimed that as a result the charge overstated cost. This was important to some eastern roads, which had enormous car-hire bills to pay as a result of the large number of foreign cars which the normal movement of freight continuously brought to their lines. To add to this burden western roads tried several times to increase the per diem charge with an incentive charge, called penalty per diem. Their attempts were warded off by the cogent argument that the charge amounted to a penalty for the normal conduct of one's business and that the payment would threaten some small roads with bankruptcy. The argument raged but was more or less academic during the period when virtually everything moved by rail and the eastern roads prospered from their heavy volume of relatively price-inelastic freight. Farmers hold their grain in elevators until they believe the price is right and then try to move a year's (or more) crop all at once. This makes an enormous surge in the demand for cars, and regulation forbids offering price incentives to smooth out the demand. The result is car shortages, much touted in the press as the result of the public-be-damned attitude of the monster railroads. The western roads blamed the eastern, educating their senators in the use of the arcane "percent of ownership on line" as a public whipping post. (Almost no one knew what the figure meant, or what it ought to be, but it sounded important.) The ritual made for good copy and good politics, and was one of the signs of the changing seasons. The whole brouhaha could have been avoided by the establishment of a car pool, but the word has always been anathema to railroad managements. Sales people believe the individual ownership makes good advertising and shipper relations. Chairmen of the board believe a pool smacks of government ownership, an outcome to be avoided at any cost. (Curiously, railroad men have always vigorously fought for private enterprise in spite of the fact that regulation has made their enterprises more bureaucratic than market-oriented.)

When the eastern roads began to lose both passengers and freight to the highway, all the problems which could conveniently be swept under the rug during the era of regulated monopoly began to hurt, and "per diem deficit" was one of the first. The western roads controlled the AAR's decisions in car service matters because of the one-car-one-vote practice. Freight cars became more sophisticated after the war, inflation followed the debasement of the currency by Congress, and the per diem rate soared. Eastern roads screamed to the ICC that it was killing them (not too much of an exaggeration), the western roads replied that the eastern roads were car thieves and besides they were inefficiently managed. The ICC, with something less than solomonic wisdom, held the line for awhile but finally permitted penalty per diem. They called it "incentive per diem" and said the extra charge would bring cars home, but it was the same old penalty imposed on the just and the unjust alike. The result took by surprise all except the defenders of low per diem. The extra charge suddenly made it very profitable to own a freight car if it could be turned loose into the maelstrom of railroad interline service. This isn't open to just anyone, because railroads will only pay per diem charges to another railroad. This obstruction was overcome by the device of leasing thousands of new cars to tiny railroads who had the magic "reporting marks" (recognized initials blessed by the AAR entitling the owner or lessee to per diem) and sending them off line. Some financial entrepreneurs bought small railroads as launching pads for the new freight cars they had just persuaded their clients to buy. There remained the problem of getting them into service, since the rules try to prevent exactly this practice, but by hook or by crook it can be done, especially when car supply is tight, and a skilled car manager can keep a car from ever coming home under certain conditions.

There is this extra heavy rental charge, you see, sir or madam, and tax advantages as well. Many a doctor, dentist, and professor became the proud owner of a freight car. The car builders loved it. At the same time Conrail (we'll tell you about Conrail later) was in such bad shape that cars got bogged down in its yards and it had to pay the extra charges. Since the poor taxpayer had to shell out for Conrail, the doctor, dentist, and professor just had another government ripoff. Finally the ICC was persuaded to see the light, Conrail got straightened out, business fell off, and the cars came home to roost. Some tiny railroads couldn't hold all their cars and had to pay storage charges.

But to go back a bit, the four standard types of freight car (box, gondola, flat, hopper) served the early railroads well, and by the time there was demand for other types the roads were in their regulated phase, able to stand serenely above the hurly-burly of the market place. The first new type to appear was the tank car, but the roads made the oil companies acquire them, giving them a small mileage allowance on each shipment to compensate for ownership cost. This arrangement was highly satisfactory to the railroads, who didn't have to worry about idle cars. The oil companies set up private car companies, whose reporting marks traditionally end in "X", and General American Tank Car Company, or GATX, is an establishment known to any train watcher. Refrigerator cars were the only other type early to come into general use. These also were supplied by private car lines, but the railroads in this case owned the car lines. Thus the fiction of not stepping out of line by offering a special type was preserved but the needs of the shippers of fruit and produce were met. Elaborate rules and charges were then established for the supply of ice or heating fuel en route and the way was opened to the feeding of the whole country with produce grown in its most fertile areas. This movement of vitamins over thousands of miles across many state lines without customs interference is undoubtedly one of the chief reasons for America's greatness, directly attributable to the wisdom of our fathers in prohibiting interference with interstate commerce. Germans and English live just as close to orange-growing country as New Yorkers do, but foreign governments with customs walls intervene, their railroads never developed the movement, and to them orange juice is a luxury, not everyman's breakfast.

Again we digress, but the fact was that during most of the railroad era freight cars were of a few standard types, and the shippers could take it or leave it. If the shipper complained that his freight didn't fit the car he was told with Procrustean hauteur to block it more carefully. If he wanted a service not named in a tariff, such as having an engine move a partially unloaded car to another door while the engine was at the plant, it would be patiently explained to him that such a favor would be illegal. Regulation required that every service offered be precisely described and priced in a formal tariff on file for all to see, and tariffs had the force of law. Without a doubt this became the most convenient excuse for not doing something a customer wanted that ever existed. It wasn't necessary to make a cost benefit decision. It wasn't possible to favor a good customer because anything done for one had to be available to all. Is it becoming apparent why three or four generations of this dulled the once eager marketing sense of railroad men?

Early freight service was so much faster and cheaper than anything which had been known that for awhile there was little stimulus to make it faster and cheaper still. Taken from the shipper's siding by an industrial switcher or a local freight train, cars were made into a train and sent in the direction of their destination. Crew runs were 100 - 150 miles, and rail lines were organized into divisions of about that length. Some companies emphasized the division, making it virtually a separate road, and some the department, a distinction of more interest to a student of management than to the general reader. In any case the whole train would be taken apart at the end of the division and cars for further movement turned over to the next division unswitched, helter-skelter, or "feathers and guts", in the time-honored railroad slang. Interchange agreements and standardization solved the greater problem of transfer of lading at interchange points, but it was a long time before railroads learned to manage loaded car movement by preblocking in such a way as to minimize reswitching.

This important improvement began to appear in the 1930s as a result of the stimulus of truck competition and the strictures of the Smoot-Hawley Depression. Not long before this, car retarders had been invented, making hump yards more efficient. Now, hump yards are merely switching, or classification yards so placed on an artificial hill, or hump, that the cars, pushed slowly over the hill and uncoupled as they reach the top, roll by gravity into the appropriate tracks for their loads' destinations. The car retarder pinched the car's wheels at strategic points under the control of an operator in a tower, thus avoiding the expense of an army of car riders who previously used the car's brakes to control it. This device considerably reduced the cost and somewhat reduced the time lost in switching. The new art of preblocking eliminated much of the switching entirely. The development of the steam locomotive, especially the so-called superpower engine, with firebox large enough to supply high horsepower in the upper speed ranges (for the buffs, one of the best examples was the Nickel Plate's stable of 2-8-4's), raised freight train speeds. Regulation controlled prices and forbade special services, but it didn't prevent competition in speed. The movement of freight, which looked so fast to the early patrons used to canals and wagons but so slow to us looking back, began to speed up in the second quarter of the twentieth century. For example, in the '30s there were eight major routes from Chicago to Boston (there were probably 150 possible combinations of individual railroads) which provided reliable third morning delivery. Trains over the fastest route arrived Boston in the afternoon of the second day, assuring delivery by the next morning even to outlying points or places difficult of access. Curiously, this route required the cooperation of four separate railroads, successfully outdistancing even the one route which was under single line control.

An important recent development is the unit train. Where large movements are contemplated there are economies to be realized by the shipment of a trainload all at once. This has long been known, and indeed should be apparent to anyone who thinks about it for a minute. Early efforts to offer unit train rates failed to receive regulatory blessing, however. Cost studies to support the application used the greater degree of equipment utilization which the process produces to show a substantial drop in unit equipment cost. This virtually self-evident postulate was, of course, the reason for the proposal. Regulatory authority, however, insisted that only historical utilization figures could be used, thus killing the idea. It should be noted that this is not a new invention, only a modest change in procedure, but even that was too much for the ICC to stomach. There was also some populist nonsense to the effect that it would be unfair to the small shipper who couldn't ship a trainload. There never was much pressure, because in a regulated monopoly who wants lower rates? Finally under the impetus of competition from other modes and after much argument it came into being. Its first use put out of business a conveyor belt for coal already in place and working, a dramatic demonstration of the efficiency of unit trains. It would be difficult to find a more impressive display of the productivity of the flanged wheel on which we based our definition of a railroad in Chapter I.

Much in the public eye in this ninth decade is TOFC/COFC. That stands for trailer-on-flat-car or container-on-flat-car, usually called piggyback. The basis of this operation is that trucks are more flexible and thus more efficient for short hauls and distribution, but rail haul is more efficient for the line haul in considerable volume. That's so simple a concept that one observing from outside might be forgiven for wondering why it is not immediately adopted for most freight movements. Unfortunately there are a number of institutional inhibitions. Incidentally, this concept is not new. In the nineteenth century farmers on Long Island loaded wagons of produce for the city on railroad flat cars. Early in the railway era British railways offered regular schedules for the movement of gentlemen's carriages. The renaissance in this century occurred on two lines in the '30s. The Chicago, North Shore & Milwaukee, an electric line, began to haul trailers between Chicago and Milwaukee, and the New Haven offered service between Boston and New York. The New Haven's service developed into two trains per day each way, but having reached that plateau, a small portion of the total market, seemed unable to grow further. No doubt there were many causes for this limitation, but the Teamsters were primarily responsible. The trucking companies who offered trailers to the railroad were allowed to do so by the Teamsters only if the trailers represented an excess over the trucking company's normal volume. At that time the alternative practice of the railroad's offering trailers direct to the shippers had not developed. About 20 years later TOFC began to appear more or less everywhere. Railroads offered a variety of plans ranging from full door-to-door service in railroad-owned trailers to mere line-haul movement of another's trailer delivered at the railroad by the shipper or another carrier. Soon TOFC grew rapidly and for distances of 800-900 miles or more the railroads attracted a respectable share of the market. That is, beyond the zone in which truck service is overnight the railroads did well - especially well in transcontinental traffic.

But most truck traffic is within the 500-mile range. Here railroads were unable to capture more than one or two percent of the market. Again the reasons were varied, but prominent among them were the railroads' lack of marketing sense and good cost analysis. Under protective regulation neither is necessary. With respect to TOFC, railroads could not grasp the importance to the customer of frequency of service, nor could they price their various services intelligently. Cost advantages resulting from higher utilization possible with greater frequency were imperfectly understood. Frequency and speed of train operation was thwarted by the traditional operating man's aversion to short trains (about which more later). Some prices were set too high to attract traffic and some so low that the traffic was handled at a loss. Price changes and experimentation were difficult under regulation because any rate (price) proposed would be challenged and suspended for months. At the same time, once established, rates became part of the sacred rate structure. In the late '70s this regulation began to be relaxed, and in 1981 it was to a considerable degree removed, but habits die hard, and railroad men used to the ways of three or four generations did not become instant marketeers. As this is written (1982) it is uncertain whether railroads can regain a substantial portion of this traffic, but growth is being accomplished in spite of the generally depressed total market.

In an artificial situation where no marketing skills are required the tremendous capability of railroad technology and railroad skills becomes apparent. During World War II truly prodigious feats were performed. In spite of shortages of everything - men, equipment, and materials - both time and volume demands far beyond all experience were met heroically. The story of the railroads' response to the challenge of World War II deserves and will be given a chapter of its own.

As an offset to our constant harping about lack of marketing skills, one example of successful exploitation of a new market should be related. When shipping lines developed the use of containers, which enormously simplified the loading and unloading of ships, it became feasible to interchange freight between ship and train far more easily than before. This opened the possibility of saving much valuable ship time in the voluminous trade between Europe and the Far East by transferring the cargo at an Atlantic port to rail movement and again at a Pacific port to another ship. The market was indeed skillfully exploited. The movement was called a land bridge, and it grew rapidly. Shipping lines benefited because their vessels could avoid the circuitous and time-consuming movement through the Panama Canal. Railroads benefited because they were offered solid trains of containers to haul, the job they do best. The market has expanded to more than the Europe - Far East trade. In addition freight is similarly moved between eastern North America and the Orient, and between western North America and Europe, these moves usually called minibridge. It is noteworthy that these developments have virtually made the Panama Canal obsolete, rendering most of the rhetoric of the politicians about that big ditch so much sound and fury.

It also makes one wonder if the ditch was worth the effort in the first place, or whether it's merely another example of the government's wasting our substance on something the free market wisely shunned. What is certain is that that other ditch, the St. Lawrence Seaway, is a complete waste of taxpayers' money. All the freight it moves could move on Canadian and U. S. railroads for less money, and its volume would go far to solve the problems of the railroads of the Northeast, of which more anon.

This leaves the current rail scene a curious mixture of accomplishment. On the one hand are considerable achievements of land bridge, unit trains of grain and coal, and similar movements of heavy volume at very low cost, displaying the inherent productivity of rail technology to the utmost. In the middle, so to speak, is TOFC/COFC, where there is both achievement in long-haul, high-volume movement, but only tentative exploration, so far, into the large medium-distance movement. At the low end is the abandonment to the motor carrier of most of the merchandise traffic, at least some of which is undoubtedly amenable to rail movement if approached with innovative attitude and marketing skill. It remains to be seen whether the current partial relaxation of regulation will foster new developments which may tend to restore the ubiquity of rail service. If it can, not only will railroads benefit, but all of us will enjoy some diminution of congestion on highways.

CHAPTER VI

THE CHALLENGE OF

WORLD WAR II

The sudden enormous increase in demand for both passenger and freight movement which World War II created, coming as it did soon after the abnormally low demand of the Smoot-Hawley Depression, presented an unprecedented challenge. The railroads became an important part of the assembly line of every war industry. They were needed to move millions of troops and vast quantities of war supplies, transporting materials for the construction of army camps, air bases, supply depots, airdromes, shipyards, and ships. They transported most of the raw materials used in munitions plants, airplane factories, and other war industries. They moved to all parts of the country and to the seaports immense quantities of implements and materials, as well as fuels and food, to keep the nation's war machine operating at maximum efficiency. More than 97% of all troops and about 90% of all Army and Navy equipment and supplies were transported by rail during the war.

The volume of passengers and freight doubled and tripled, and the enormous demands of military movement were superimposed on even that burden. Military movements were uniquely exacting in kind as well as in size. Suddenly to be confronted with a demand for 12-15 trains of 20 sleeping cars and 20-30 flat cars each (to move one division) imposed an undreamed-of task on a railroad staff accustomed to reasonably orderly and predictable demands of far smaller magnitude. A few numbers will show the extent of the effort. From December, 1941, to August, 1945, a total of 113,891 special troop trains were operated for distances ranging up to 3000 miles, involving 303,003 coach trips, 511,385 sleeping car trips, 142,706 baggage and kitchen car trips, and 193,784 freight car trips. During this period the railroads transported 43,700,000 members of the armed forces in special troop or hospital trains or in special cars attached to regular trains, an average monthly movement of 971,110 troops. These figures do not include millions of trips made by military personnel traveling singly or in small groups on duty or furlough or returning home after discharge. It is interesting to compare the average monthly movement with that of World War I, which was 475,450, or slightly less than one half. To accomplish this almost no new locomotives and cars could be obtained because the plants which made them were busy turning out military materiel. Few men could be hired because of enlistment and conscription into the armed forces. Very little material for repair was available.

The surge of traffic from the year before and from the bottom of the depression is clearly shown in the following Table:

Year	Ton-miles (millions)	Passenger miles (millions)
1932	233,977	16,971
1940	373,253	23,762
1944	737,246	95,549
Increase -		
1940-44	97.5%	302.1%
1932-44	315.1%	463.0%

Source: Association of American Railroads

The job was done by the development of co-operation and centralized planning unheard of before and since. The almost devastating experience of World War I, when the federal government seized all railroads with nearly disastrous results, was well remembered, and this memory served to prevent a repetition. This time the centralized planning was done, not by the government but by the Association of American Railroads, which established a military liaison department within a few days of Pearl Harbor. Later on the government set up something called the Office of Defense Transportation, whose actions were largely cosmetic, but which did forbid the wasteful use of box cars for small shipments, thus providing a defense against shippers' pressure for favors. The AAR's new military liaison depart-ment, however, arranged with the Department of Defense to have all demands for transport channeled through it. Each railroad designated an officer who knew his line's capabilities in detail (usually the car service officer named in Chapter V) to deal with the AAR military office and with his counterpart in other railroads' organizations. Thus the confusion of the earlier conflict was nipped in the bud. Men worked prodigious hours - many of them 16 hours a day for days on end. The utilization of equipment was tremendously increased by meeting the increased demand with good equipment manage-ment. Locomotives and cars long out of service were patched up and put to use. The job was done, and no ship ever was delayed awaiting its lading. One measure of the magnitude of the job is that for every soldier sent overseas the Army sent initially six tons of equipment and supplies, followed by an additional ton each month. Another measure is that in the three years from August, 1942, to August, 1945, some 294 million tons of Army supplies were moved by railroad, 26 million by motor carriers, and 4 million by inland waterways

The comparison of the accomplishments of the railroads in World War I, when they were seized by and operated by the government, and World War II, when they were operated by their own managements, is both startling and revealing. In 1944 about the same miles of track were in operation as in 1918, but the roads had 33% less locomotives, 24% less freight cars, 30% less passenger cars, and 23% less employees. With this sharply reduced plant they moved 82% more ton-miles and 124% more passenger-miles. All of the productivity statistics (*e.g.* net ton-miles per freight train hour, which went up 141%) increased enormously. Average revenue per ton-mile was 12% higher, but average revenue per passenger mile was 28% lower. During the first war passenger revenue per mile increased 51% and freight revenue per mile 80%. During the second war the average revenue figures changed only slightly, one up 2% and the other down a like amount. The horrible congestion of the first w, caused by such actions as shipping a carload of anchors to the site of a shipyard before the shipyard was built, was prevented in the second by the cooperation of the agencies described above. The bottom line figure is revealing. In the first war the railroads ran deficits which cost the taxpayers some two million dollars per day. In the second war they paid income taxes of over three million dollars a day.

The most dramatic example of the performance of the railroads in World War II was the movement of oil, a problem which had not existed in the earlier conflict. In the years preceding the second war oil was in great demand in the Northeast, both for gasoline and for home heating, having by that time largely supplanted coal. This oil was moved by ocean tanker, never by rail, whether because the railroads' lack of marketing sense had caused failure to exploit the market or because oil companies preferred to use tankers, which they could control, sparks many a controversy. The present pipe line network had not developed. A small number of tank cars were in use moving oil a few miles inland from various ports, but rail movement from the Texas oilfields to the Northeast was a mere trickle of 11,250 barrels a day just before the war. The German U-Boat Command saw the vulnerability of tanker movement and promptly sank most of them, rendering the coastal waters completely unsafe and precipitating a crisis. Both war plants and homes needed that oil. The railroads were called on again, in this instance to do something they had never done in any significant quantity. What tank cars there were (there was neither time nor materials to build new ones) were commandeered, locomotives were found virtually in scrap heaps, a schedule of solid oil trains was established, some 75 being dispatched daily for the long haul, and the unbelieveable was somehow accomplished. Movement expanded to over a million barrels daily, almost a hundredfold increase. Oil trains, in addition to all the military movements and the swollen freight and passenger volume, rolled from Texas to the Northeast, factories continued to produce, and nobody froze.

There were other shifts of tonnage from water routes to railroads during the war because of the submarine menace and the transfer of steamships to other services. Among the important tonnage movements taken over in whole or in part by the railroads were sugar from Cuba, bauxite and other ores from South America, phosphate rock from Florida, sulphur from Texas, and lumber from the South and West. Large quantities of coal which formerly moved by rail and water moved all-rail. The need for every available vessel on the Great Lakes for the movement of iron ore caused much bulk traffic, including coal and grain, to be diverted to the railroads. The wartime closing of the Panama Canal, demonstrating even then its redundancy discussed in a previous chapter, shifted to the railroads the 27 million tons of commerce formerly moved through the big ditch.

It is said that the improvement of the taste of meat which cooking accomplishes was discovered when a house burned down and accidentally roasted a pig. The point has frequently been made that once the method is discovered it shouldn't be necessary to burn the house down in order to enjoy roast pork. Similarly it shouldn't be necessary to go through a devastating war to demonstrate the enormous capacity and productivity of the technology of the flanged wheel which we used as our definition of a railroad in the opening chapter.

CHAPTER VII

LOVE-HATE RELATIONSHIP

In its earliest beginnings the railroad inspired fear, awe, admiration, and unprecedented excitement. It soon became recognized as the *sine qua non* of commercial development. Indeed, it is still apparent that the villages which remain villages are those which were not served by rail. By the time it became established as the accepted means of transport it came to permeate the life of every town as well as that of the cities. The railroad station* was where things happened. Not only were persons' comings and goings to be noted there, but the telegraph, bringer of world news, was there. The fascinating spectacle of the locomotive was there to be seen. Mail and newspapers arrived there. The express car and the local freight brought the town's supplies and took its exports. There was activity at night and all day Sunday. Every snowfall was first cleared away from its environs. It was a symbol of dependability and a link with the world which prevented somnolent retrogression. Many a small business depended for its custom on the stream of passengers and onlookers who came and went. Everybody loved the railroad station even as he loved to ride on the train.

The remote managers of the railroad were something else again. They were faceless, rich, altogether

---

*Never "train station". How that neologism came into being is a mystery. Probably in the decline of passenger service the bus station was more familiar, and "train station" appeared by association therewith.

too powerful. They set the schedules of trains; they hired and fired. They had control of vast resources. Of course the productivity which was the central aspect of the railroad produced enormous wealth. Equally of course in a free society most of that wealth redounded to people in general, increasing living standards for everybody. Inevitably, however, a tiny portion of that wealth, which in spite of being a tiny portion was as an absolute sum very large, found its way into the hands of a few. Some vast fortunes were made. Now, envy is a natural reaction, and most of us have little trouble convincing ourselves that we could have made similar fortunes if only Lady Luck had smiled on us. Our feelings made us eager to believe the stories which many a journalist wrote about Robber Barons. Only the more discriminating recognize that the epithet is deserved only by some predators, who were like jackals stalking the real builders and leaders of the industry. Leo Rosten, writing in the *Saturday Review* in late 1976 on popular examples of false information, has caught a piece of the truth:

> Mathew Josephson coined the "Robber Barons" sobriquet, and his book of that name has become some sort of classic. Josephson electrified and outraged us with indisputable data about these shameless buccaneers of capitalism, who lined their pockets by picking ours.

> Today, historians with no unground axes or bleeding hearts reveal that these predators pulled off their most scandalous capers only through collusion with, and crucial assistance from, agencies of government. Public officials were the ones who created and protected the wolves.

Railroads, for instance, got stupendous subsidies from federal or state laws, then farmed out the costly construction or expansion to phony subcontractors: themselves. The notorious Erie Gang (Gould, Fisk, Drew) made their bonanzas through secret stock manipulations only because New York's legislature was controlled by the public servants whom the villains bribed. The Californians known as the Big Four (Stanford, Hopkins, Crocker, Huntington) operated through shmeared puppets in Sacramento: the Central Pacific Railroad became one of the most brazen flimflams in our history - because the Robber Barons were given a government monopoly on certain rail routes. At one point, you could send freight to San Francisco by ship, all the way around South America, for much less than the legally protected Central Pacific charged to haul it.

To nail the case down, compare the records of competitive and "unprotected" railroads. Vanderbilt and Hill and the railroads they ran without any government payola or monopoly were more profitable to their stockholders and much cheaper to shippers than was the Central Pacific. The Eastern empire-builders did not steal a dime from the taxpayers - in "subsidies".

It is worth noting that the net effect was well on the positive side. As for the jackals, they preyed on rich men and brought down with them only the individuals who hoped to make a fast buck by following them. The builders created a wealth-producing structure far greater than anything the jackals could destroy. The net inheritance from their combined efforts was of service to society for well over a century before its destruction by a different kind of jackal. Nevertheless, the builders and jackals alike were feared and hated.

Curiously the moguls didn't think of themselves as powerful. As we saw in Chapter III, they feared the competition of the young upstarts within the industry, and wisely so. If people had known how vulnerable the supposed mighty were, we might have avoided the stultification which resulted, but sensational journalism and envy had opened the door for the counterproductive efforts of the populists. The result, coupled with the love for the technology and its apparent economic benefits, led to the worst kind of worship of the status quo. For two or three generations it became received wisdom that what was bad for the railroads was bad for the country.

Nevertheless, they were still rich, and so must be evil. They were easy to tax, because the very large value added by transport in the case of all manufactured products made the demand for transport highly inelastic. That is, if the cost of transport represents one half of one percent of a product's delivered price (not an uncommon ratio) then even doubling the price of transport would only increase the product's price by one half of one percent. At the same time price competition, which would have held down even such trifling increases, was prevented by regulation. Taxes, therefore, levied on railroads by all levels of government, were easily passed along and completely hidden in their effect. Worthy school boards and corrupt politicians alike rejoiced in so lucrative a source of revenue and of course became as dependent on it as any heroin addict on his drug. This dependence led to one aspect of many instances of uneven governmental policies toward competing modes of transport. South Station, Boston, regularly paid millions of dollars in taxes to the city. Logan Airport, which serves the same function, pays none.

At the state level it became apparent to railroads early in their development that their technology and devices fascinated legislatures to the point that the solons couldn't keep their hands off them. Not only taxes, but a plethora of restrictive laws, conflicting, counter-productive, and just plain silly, were enacted. The most infamous is the law requiring that when two trains approached a crossing each must stop and neither might proceed until the other had passed. In order to nip as many as possible of these dangerous nuisances in the bud it was considered wise to maintain lobbies at any seat of government. Although probably never as strong as some of today's lobbies, they were to some degree effective, and this effectiveness was well worked over by many a journalist in search of a story. The verb "to railroad", meaning to force a motion through a supposedly deliberative body, was added to our language.

A combination of circumstances and attitudes brought about the establishment of separate railroad police forces. First there was the wave of train robberies featuring Jesse James, which public authorities were powerless to prevent. They were put down by a private agency engaged by the railroads, and this was how Pinkerton's got its start. Then there was the fact that any railroad, even in the more densely populated East, owned property scattered so far and wide that much of it was beyond the habitual patrol area of the authorities. In addition there were attitudes of envy and even fear which put railroads outside of police protection. Jesse James was something of a hero whose exploits were as avidly devoured by newspaper readers as airplane highjackers in more recent times, but with noticeably more sympathy. Railroads were big enough to take care of themselves, people thought, and cops have more important things to do. The result was the establishment by each railroad of its own police force, a tough and challenging job which produced a truly elite corps. They were treated coldly by regular police and with aloofness by railroaders, who were never sure they weren't management spies. All this made for a lonely job, but they met the challenge well. Some roads put them in uniform and some not, but many of them showed a bravery and a contempt for threats which was a comfort in lonely reaches of a remote railroad yard in the middle of the night.

The inelasticity of demand explained above, together with lack of competition, made feasible substantial expenses by railroads, leading to the usual combined reactions of admiration and envy. In northern cities while everyone was vigorously shoveling snow after a storm he was apt to notice that the railroad station's premises were cleaned up early, long before the city cleaned up the streets. In the event of even a minor accident railroad claim agents appeared miraculously with pockets stuffed with cash, eager to settle claims. It was at the same time good to have so substantial a citizen for a neighbor but obnoxious that anyone should be so wealthy. Certainly the last thing any such entity needed was protection from competition.

On the contrary, when the swollen traffic of World War I and the inept management of the government congested the railroads, it became a patriotic cry to ship by truck and save a car for Uncle Sam. Thus did the fledgling truck lines get their start. As they grew in later years they found the railroads easy prey. Their operations were theoretically more expensive, because a truck hauls so much less than a train, but the rigidities inherent in both the technology and institutions of railroading destroyed this advantage. The technology was such that the all-important productivity could only be produced by putting cars into trains with others going in the same direction, involving expense and delay. The institutional encumbrances were worse. Management had been concerned with internal cost-saving improvements, with some competition at common points with other railroads who were subject to the same rigidities, but not for a couple of generations with the development of a market or adaptation to a customer's needs. Car sizes, train sizes, procedures such as switching the customer's siding, prices, and every criterion had been developed in such a way as to maximize railroad efficiency and were set forth in a series of tariffs which had the force of law, as railroaders liked to remind everybody. Any effort to adjust any of this to a customer's convenience would be frowned on not only by railroad management, but by the federal government, who accepted responsibility "in the public interest" for guarding the inviolability of the sacred rate structure.

The inviolability of the rate structure worked both ways. Not only were rate reductions prohibited, but rate increases, even if clearly supportable by increases in cost beyond management's control, were delayed, cut down, or sometimes denied altogether in a spirit of populism. (Electric utilities are today suffering the same devastating experience.) Albro Martin, in his exhaustive and penetrating *Enterprise Denied* describes the dismal failure of regulation in the early years of this century. He says (page 354): "Railroad regulation failed in this period for two principal reasons: first, because the philosophies and policies of archaic Progressivism were applicable to problems and conditions which no longer existed, and second, because the Commission simply did not constitute the fearless, impartial, and wise body which regulation presupposed."* He describes in detail the tremendous increase in volume with which the railroads were faced, so great as to require massive infusions of capital to build up capacity. This capital, which investors were formerly so eager to put into railroading, was not forthcoming because the populist politics of the era effectively prevented the ICC

---

*Albro Martin, *Enterprise Denied*, Columbia University Press, 1971.

from permitting necessary rate increases. These increases were necessary because inflation was rapidly escalating railroad costs in spite of a steady 5% per annum improvement in productivity. With costs going up and revenues (in constant dollars) declining, the roads' financial results looked dismal, and investors would have none of it. Martin marks the beginning of the decline in the railroad industry's physical and financial condition at this point even though it was not apparent to the casual observer until much later.

The rigidities of the labor unions were even more severe. Exasperated by the ferocious demands of a 24-hour service in a time of rapid growth and fearful of the devastating effect on jobs of cyclical changes in volume, they had used the power which protective regulation gave them to freeze job patterns in every conceivable way. A switching move could not be made by a "road" crew except under severely restricted circumstances. Geographical boundaries of work and enfeoffment of jobs were delineated. In the face of these and other restrictions any effort at adjusting to the market (as appeared much later when changed circumstances made it desirable) became in many cases impossible. For example, a railroad attempting to win from a motor carrier a specific move of only a few miles ran into this difficulty. Technologically a small engine could be dispatched to move a few cars a short distance at a cost which would make it competitive with truck movement. Institutionally, however, it was necessary to pay one five-man crew to pick up the cars (that's switching) another to move it to the first division point (fixed arbitrarily and happening to intervene in this case) another to move to destination, and another to place the cars. One crew would be happy to do all the work if all the crews were paid.

Motor carriers, free of such restrictions and at first unregulated, were perceived as more efficient because of this flexibility. This made it easy politically to justify spending huge sums of highway money to provide them with their rights-of-way. As time went by and railroads began to decline many people saw the injustice of this, but in our system of pressure-group government it is virtually impossible to correct such a mistake. To the truck operators and the Teamsters Union members who work for them it is perceived as a matter of millions of dollars expense if they had to pay their share of highway construction and maintenance costs. They therefore bring concerted pressure on congressmen effectively to prevent any such change in the status quo. The far greater number of auto drivers whose gasoline tax might be somewhat reduced by such action perceive it, if they perceive it at all, as a rather minor concern, not likely to have any great influence on their votes for congressmen or anyone else. The possible effect on general taxation is even more vague. The irony of this example of the ineptitude of pressure-group government is that the fears of the truckers and teamsters are almost certainly groundless. As in the case of railroad taxation explained above, the freight charges of trucks are also inelastic. Such charges form a small part of the cost of the goods moved, and the increase in them necessary to defray the highway costs would be virtually invisible in the delivered price of the goods themselves. Theoretically it would remove a price advantage over the railroads now (unjustly) held by the trucks, with resulting loss of competitive advantage. In fact, however, it is eminently clear from experience that the railroads cannot win merchandise traffic from the trucks by lowering rates. Even under regulation such experiments have been tried, but hardly a dent is ever thus made in the trucks' control of the merchandise market except in the rare instances where it is accompanied by dramatic service improvement.

One of the reasons why appropriate charges cannot be levied for the use of public highways illustrates a fundamental failing of governmental control of economic matters. The charges are called taxes. Thus when an increase in the "gas tax" is called for the cry of politicians and the media is that taxes must be reduced, not increased. Now the trouble is that such a specific user charge, at least to the extent that it is directed to the covering of a specific cost, has a wholly different effect from an increase in, say, the income tax. The latter has a depressing effect on the economy in general, especially on capital formation. The user charge, on the other hand, affects only the use of a specific resource, reducing its use and/or providing for its maintenance and renewal. In that sense it is not a tax at all. Politicians and the media cannot understand this, of course, and therefore it is politically virtually impossible to levy charges which would cause those who enjoy the benefits of a resource to pay for it.

The distortion caused by the institutional burdens have reached the point of virtually nullifying the technological advantage of the railroad. Thus at the time of the partial deregulation of 1981 it had come to pass that a motor carrier owner-operator, paying no wages and burdened with no union restrictions, paying less than his share of the cost of his right-of-way, could move a trailer for a lesser charge than a rail carload rate. This in spite of the fact that his right-of-way is inherently more expensive to build and maintain, he must supply a driver (himself) and motive power for each vehicle moved, and his fuel consumption is much higher. Obviously without the artificial advantages resulting from institutional restraints and subsidies his services would cost more by an order of magnitude.

A similar misallocation of funds occurs in the development of inland waterways. Since the country's earliest days the most effective lobby in Washington has been the Army Corps of Engineers. They successfully urge Congress to spend huge sums in the dredging of rivers and the digging of ditches, using estimates of costs and benefits which repeatedly have been shown false. The eagerness with which Congressmen engage in rhetoric and log-rolling in support of these ventures has become legendary. Arguments about the desirability of free natural waterways have no bearing on the construction of expensive artificial waterways. The ultimate and unanswerable argument is that if their use were economically justified they would be built without taxpayers' money. Nevertheless, the fact is that they are lavishly built and used by the barge operators. Until 1981 they were used without charge; in that year a token "tax" was assessed which represents a small portion of the cost. It should be remembered that the water carriers are not disciples of Huck Finn riding down the Mississippi on a raft but substantial businesses carrying bulk cargoes shipped by large corporations.

Before the development of the motor truck and the diesel-powered tow-boats the railroads were supreme. Regulation served only to solidify their position and render them less sensitive to market needs. When the motor truck appeared the first reaction of the railroads was a cry for regulation. This was in the Smoot-Hawley Depression, when government interference in the marketplace was rampant, and regulation came to pass. It had been the railroad man's hope that this would solve the problem, but it completely failed to do so. As we explained in Chapter III, the regulation of the two modes was very uneven. The provision of rights-of-way by government, with such charges as there were made on a use basis, gave the motor carriers a completely different type of cost structure. As a result, comparison of rail and truck costs in any specific instance became impossible for lack of a common denominator. There were other differences, the most important being that motor carriers were never required to maintain all services to all comers, a frequent cause of financial drain to railroads. If a railroad tried to compete with a truck by offering a reduced rate, regulatory authority would often deny it by finding the railroad not to be the "true low-cost carrier", a designation purely arbitrary, based on the impossible cost comparison mentioned above. No one can recall a similar denial to a motor carrier. Regulation, so far from solving the problem, became an important part of it.

The inequities of government's uneven policies had a deadening effect on railroad management which can only be likened to the psychological effect of segregation on minorities. Indeed, John Barriger called railroads the niggers of American industry. It is well known that if one repeatedly tells a person or a group that he is inferior he will begin to believe it.* Railroad men, having been for a century in an exalted position, suffered a psychological depression under the government's misguided acts. Once every little boy wanted to be an engineer when he grew up. Even as late as World War II the accomplishments of the railroads were widely recognized, and railroad men occupied a place of honor just below the military heroes themselves. Then it became received wisdom that trucks were more efficient, and therefore that it was correct for them to receive government favors. The illogic of this should have been evident, because if they were more efficient they should have less need of government favors, but politics and logic rarely mix. The physical capabilities of the respective technologies won't support the contention anyway, but the psychological effect of the error caused a compounding of the difficulties of railroad managements in coping with their marketing problems. Not only had they been so shielded from the real

---

*The U. S. Supreme Court in its decision outlawing segregation by race in public schools, *Brown* v. *Board of Education of Topeka, Kansas,* 347 U.S. 483 (1954), based its decision on this fact rather than on precedent.

world as to know little about marketing, now they had the added burden of an inferiority complex. They were persuaded that their only hope for meeting competition, since their service was bad, was to lower rates. Unfortunately it didn't work, because for a great deal of high-value freight the customer doesn't want low rates as much as he wants good service. Technologically the railroad can provide superb service, as a few unfortunately isolated examples have shown, but it was a rare railroad management that saw that, even when demonstrations made it evident.

Railroads, which for two or three generations had been money machines, used to adequate revenue virtually guaranteed by protective regulation, fell on hard times. The original productivity of their technology was still there, but it was so encumbered with institutional burdens that it was vulnerable to any competition and doubly so to a competition which was favored by government largesse. To add to the industry's troubles, even its clumsy efforts (made clumsy by the stultification of protective regulation) to adjust to changing times by price changes or the withdrawal of unused services were thwarted by regulators who were even more hidebound. This dismal descent was most dramatic in the passenger business. Passengers deserted the trains, as Chapter IV relates, but the trains continued to run. Heroic efforts following World War II to win passengers back were to no avail. The deficits which resulted amounted to some $300 million annually and increased as time went on. At first these deficits were cross-subsidized by freight revenue, but as the freight business suffered from the causes outlined above this became impossible.

In the Northeast both of these problems were much worse than in the West and South. The freight business in the Northeast consisted largely of commodities readily carried by truck, and passenger service was far more intensive and costly. When freight revenue could no longer sustain the passenger losses effort was made to keep afloat by cutting back on maintenance. The inevitable result was the rapid deterioration of the property. This made service slower and uncomfortable, hastening the loss of business. The passenger station, once the proud symbol of wealth, security, dependability, and public service, became a crumbling derelict, home for drop-outs from society. Passenger trains, once fast and luxurious, became slow, decrepit, and uncomfortable. To make matters worse, much of the northeastern railroads' traffic simply disappeared. Coal for home heating and industrial fuel was displaced by oil, which moved by pipeline or water. Heavy freight- producing industry, e.g. textiles, moved south.

All of these difficulties were summarized expertly in a 1973 report to the government by the National Council of Economic Research as follows:

External -
1. Limited access to capital (low earnings)
2. Trends in intermodal competition
3. Shifts in regional transport demand
4. Unbalanced federal investment policies
5. Adverse regulatory policies

Internal -
1. Operating inefficiencies
2. Low service quality
3. Resistance to change by (a) management (b) labor
4. Lack of innovation in (a) marketing (b) pricing (c) operating practices.

Efforts to cope with the disaster led to the ill-fated Penn Central merger. Every knowledgeable and disinterested observer known to this writer agreed that such a move was ill-advised. It combined the two largest northeastern railroads (Pennsylvania and New York Central), who suffered from almost identical problems. Thus their combination merely doubled the difficulty. Conceivably merger of each with one of the coal roads, whose steady traffic in a bulk commodity and freedom from passenger service had kept them strong, might have worked. Merger of the New York Central with the Chesapeake and Ohio, and of the Pennsylvania with the Norfolk and Western, had often been suggested, but neither got far. The only reason ever heard was the possibility of personality clashes in high places. In any case, Penn Central went through. The ICC, guiltridden because of the condition of its wards, seized on the vain hope, and made it worse by insisting on the inclusion of the New Haven, its worst problem child.

Penn Central was soon bankrupt, and the problem was all the worse. Virtually every northeastern railroad was now bankrupt except the coal roads named above, and the government faced the brutal necessity of doing something about the mess it had made. Why not forget it? Isn't the natural working of a free market supposed to weed out the obsolete and defunct? The problem here is that the free market had not been allowed to operate for almost a century. The railroad technology was far from obsolete. What was defunct was their institutional structure. The railroads were still very much needed to handle traffic which even their highly favored competitors could not physically move. Much industry would have been literally stopped without rail service. Proof of this technological competence is to be found in the fact that where institutional restraints were absent, private money with no axe to grind chose to build railroads to handle substantial transportation jobs. Thus in the United States we had the paradox of a device so technically sound as to be indispensible going to wrack and ruin because of institutional problems. Since those institutional problems were the result of governmental action it was up to Congress to do something about it. If Congress had left it alone in 1887 there probably would have been no problem.

Congress' answer was to pass a massive bill which set up a new bureaucracy, the United States Railroad Administration (USRA) and a new railroad, the Consolidated Railroad Corporation (Conrail), to take over and operate the rail properties of Penn Central and all the other bankrupt northeastern railroads. One of them, the Boston and Maine, held out, declined the government money, and elected to try to emerge from bankruptcy on its own. USRA enlisted the services of competent railroad men and attacked the problem of the appropriate route structure for Conrail with vigor. Various possible arrangements were studied. One which would have corrected the mistake of Penn Central by separating the two major railroads (thus permitting renewal of the idea of merger of each with a strong coal road) was unfortunately rejected. Apparently it was thought unwise to nullify a prior action even though that action had led to disaster. It also appeared to be impracticable to program the computer to be imaginative regarding arrangements for freight car movement which would have minimized inter-change under such an arrangement. This was important because "interchange" automatically rings up extra cost on the computer. Another arrangement which would have provided some competition in the area involved turning over certain lines to viable railroads, leaving Conrail essentially intact, but somewhat slimmed down and not in a monopolistic position. This was the first choice of USRA, but failed of implementation because the unions would not accept the terms offered. The railroads which were to take over portions of the bankrupt lines insisted that the men accept the working rules in effect on their lines. The men insisted that the rules in effect on the bankrupt lines be maintained. The impasse could not be resolved, and the plan fell through. USRA was then forced to fall back on its second choice, which was the amalgamation of all the bankrupt lines into a single Conrail except the B&M, mentioned above.

Conrail struggled manfully with an Augean mess, but required vast sums of government money for the first several years. This money, understandably deplored by many who object to government profligacy, was nevertheless well spent on the massive rehabilitation effort made necessary by the devastating effects, described above, of several years of undermaintenance in an effort to deal with financial stringency. It was a trying time, but it was successful. After years of struggle, Conrail's service began to improve. There were marketing men on Conrail who perceived the opportunities which deregulation would open up. They made it clear that the only way for Congress to end the flow of funds into its new child was to loosen the regulatory bonds. Finally the Staggers Act of 1980 did to a considerable degree reduce the regulation of railroads, and improvement began slowly to appear in the industry. Nowhere was this more apparent than in Conrail. Its management was greatly strengthened at the same time by the installation of a competent and experienced railroad man as chairman. Furthermore, the restrictions imposed by labor in monopoly days began to be relaxed somewhat. Labor showed signs of perceiving that rules designed to protect jobs could be counterproductive if they had the effect of putting the employer out of business. As a result of deregulation, a prompt response to it by innovative marketing, improved management, and enlightened labor, Conrail actually operated in the black in 1981.

Meanwhile the B&M proved the wisdom of its aloofness by making great strides toward reorganization. Without the benefit of the kind of government funding which

Conrail enjoyed, B&M's young and vigorous management rehabilitated the line and put it on a sound basis. Relaxation of some of the more onerous labor restrictions were won in arbitration largely because of penetrating economic analysis made by transportation faculty members in the area. The lines used in Boston's commuter service were sold to the state agency which had taken responsibility for the service, the proceeds enabling B&M to pay off its bondholders. As this is written (1982) they are in the process of being taken over by Guildford Transportation, a new company which bought the Maine Central and will probably buy the Delaware and Hudson, thus putting together a system which will run from Bangor to Buffalo, giving Conrail something like the competition which USRA and others had hoped to arrange.

It seems fair to say now that there is reason to hope that the worst of the railroads' decline is over. It is far from a foregone conclusion, however, because there are two very real dangers. For one thing there are many who strive to revert to regulation, crying for protection from an obsolete concept of rail monopoly. The ICC is still in existence, and there is still plenty of scope for populist pressure. For another not all railroad men are comfortable with their new freedom. At a time of depressed economy, those who need it can find a new scapegoat in deregulation. Nevertheless, a great blow for freedom has been struck, and with courage and a bit of luck our freight railroads may serve us well for a long time to come. Passenger service is another matter. Amtrak acts like the government agency which it in effect is. It fails dismally to operate the kind of ultra-high-speed service which the Northeast corridor needs and spends huge sums on badly-designed new equipment for slow trains across the country.

The Canadian experience has been a source of inspiration all through the struggle for deregulation. Canada has always had a more enlightened policy toward its railroads than has the United States, and in 1967 Canadian railroads were largely deregulated. The same prophecies of doom were heard, and there was a similar learning period for railroad management to get used to their new freedom. That period is now well over, however, the dire events prophesied have not taken place, and Canada now has strong railroads serving its economy well.

Not that all of our northern neighbor's troubles are over. There is still a peculiar political blight called Crows Nest Pass grain rates. The gist is that Canadian railroads are required to handle grain at the rates which were in effect in the nineteenth century, at, as might be imagined, a very considerable loss. Farmers like it, of course, and farmers have great political clout. It is to be hoped that somehow this burden may be lifted. Passenger service is in the hands of a government agency named "Via", which is much like Amtrak. In spite of all these problems, however, the substantial success of Canadian deregulation gives rise to hope that the United States may experience a similar rebirth. The success will be severely limited, however, if our governments continue their policy of showering favors on other modes while taxing railroads.

CHAPTER VIII

WHAT MIGHT HAVE BEEN

However futile as a means of reversing the course of history, some indulgence in the speculation of what might have been is perhaps justified as a way of judging the wisdom of past policies and actions. To begin such an exercise let's look at passenger train speeds. In the last decade of the nineteenth century an American type (4-4-0) locomotive hauled the Empire State Express of the New York Central and Hudson River Railroad at 112 miles per hour, Engineer Hogan up. Of course this was unique, indeed startlingly so, but it established a capability for speeds still considered remarkable almost a century later. There were other, less well publicized, isolated examples of such ultra-high-speed bursts. What is noteworthy is that nothing happened, like the dog that did not bark in the night. It seems inconceivable that in a climate of competitive enterprise this capability would not have been developed, improved, and disseminated to a considerable area. In the safety of a government-protected cartel, however, in an industry where competition was a dirty word, it was easy to apply the damper. High speed increases maintenance expense, and what good can it do? We have all the passengers already. Articles in the trade press of the time solemnly forecast passenger traffic trends exactly parallel to population forecasts. This in an industry which had demonstrated hardly two generations previously the enormous extent to which demand for transport could be stimulated by substantial improvement in service! Parenthetically, the recent high-speed services in other countries have shown again that most of the increase in travel attributable to them has come not from competing modes but from increase in demand.

The danger of competition from another railroad, the only possible source at that time, was easily put down. Another road's management was equally glad to keep maintenance cost down and equally blind to the developmental possibilities. Evidence of this is to be found in almost any book of the period, but there is one plain indication that is generally known. In that same decade when Mr. Hogan showed what could be done, the New York Central established an 18-hour train between New York and Chicago called the Twentieth Century Limited, destined to become the world's most famous train. The Pennsylvania Railroad, the only competitor with the necessary capability, matched it with the Pennsylvania Special, soon after that renamed the Broadway Limited. Now this speed (an average of some 53 miles per hour) was well below the mark which had just been set, but even so modest a schedule was too much for the ultra-conservative managements, and they agreed to slow their fastest trains to 20 hours, a schedule maintained for 30 years. Under the pressure of the depression and air competition the schedule was finally shortened in the 1930s to 16 hours. In the following decade the New York Central even made the eastbound schedule 15 1/2 hours, but of course it was too little and too late. The capital starvation begun in 1913 by unwise regulation and the Smoot-Hawley Depression combined to deny the resources for real structural improvements, and the jets ruled the skies.

What else might have happened? Well, if research and development had proceeded as we expect them to in normally competitive enterprise we certainly would have seen the 112 miles per hour of 1893 become 150 miles per hour in the next 30 years and become commonplace. This is the speed recently presented to the world with much fanfare by the French in the form of their TGV (for très grande vitesse, or ultra high speed). Now 150 miles per hour is faster than a DC-3 can fly, and there is no reason, therefore, to expect that the DC-3 would ever have carried a passenger over routes where the potential demand was great enough to justify a high-speed rail line. It would have been very useful as a feeder service in less densely populated areas. Similarly the automobile would not have invaded the dense, medium-distance markets such as Boston - New York. A glance down a column of figures listing by years the total number of rail passengers in that market shows clearly that the drop came in the same year in which it became possible to drive between those cities faster than train time. With two-hour train service this wouldn't have happened.

A 1967 study for the now defunct New England Regional Commission developed every detail of an ultra-high-speed rail service between Boston and New York. It called for a revised route, using the original Boston and Providence route through East Providence and the existing tunnel, and a wholly new line from Providence to a point just north of New Haven. Curiously the new line would have disturbed very little, the population in the parts of Rhode Island and eastern Connecticut well back from the shore being so much sparser than where the railroad is now. This new construction, together with the necessary improvements on the rest of the line would have cost $600 million at the time, but could have paid off its indebtedness in 30 years with a fare of eight dollars (coach) or sixteen dollars in parlor cars. The contemplated service was 14-car electric trains, hourly, increasing in a decade as the traffic grew to every 15 minutes in the rush hour, every 30 minutes throughout the day. The elapsed time was set at two hours 20 minutes from South Station, Boston, to Grand Central Terminal, New York, with stops at Back Bay, Route 128, Providence, and a highway interchange point outside New York such as New

Rochelle or Rye. Although not covered in the study it was apparent that a very short branch would connect Hartford with the line, permitting similar service between Connecticut cities and New York. In the light of this possibility it is the more ironic that political voices in Connecticut were vociferous against the proposal at the time. Don't let our state be desecrated for the sake of service to those outlanders from Boston and Providence, was the cry.

Not only is it easy to imagine that this high-speed capability might have come about in a less inhibited climate, it is equally important to remember that service would not have continued in areas which couldn't support it. Forcing railroads by law to continue service in areas better served by other means was as important a dampening effect on development as was the lack of entrepreneurship in more fertile fields. Railroads did in fact establish air lines and bus companies, but ownership of the former was specifically prohibited and the latter severely curtailed. The trains which they were to replace, meanwhile, were required to operate with full crew but virtually no passengers. If freedom had prevailed it's not difficult to imagine high-speed trains stopping at airports to connect with flight service to points beyond densely populated areas. The Boston and Maine, serving Northern New England, actually did start an air line, and in the pre-jet era of relatively slow airplanes they surely would have connected with any high-speed trains from New York to Boston. Later the Congress in its infinite wisdom decided that it is sinful for a railroad to own an air line, and that was the end of that effort. The coordinated air service we're here postulating would have been expensive, but busses would have provided a cheaper connecting service for those who preferred economy to speed. Substitution of busses in the areas where there was insufficient volume for efficient use of rail technology would have released resources to more productive use. Under these conditions airport location would have been much less traumatic than it has been because with well-coordinated high-speed rail service to a downtown station the airport could be virtually anywhere along the rail line.

Between New York and Washington similar arrangements would certainly have been made. Connecting air service with DC-3's for points beyond would have extended fast service to many southern cities. Of course as airplanes developed and the jet, faster than any high-speed train, appeared, the passengers from New York to either Northern New England or southern cities would have begun taking the plane all the way, but the New York - Boston and the New York - Washington passengers would not, because at the train speeds we're postulating there's no advantage to going out to the airport for so short a journey. The loss of the connecting passengers would have had some negative effect on the rail volume, but probably it would have been offset by growth. The growth which high-speed service always generates, incidentally, would have brought increasing numbers of people into and through downtown terminals, avoiding the urban decay which has resulted from the decline in rail passengers which actually occurred.

Other areas of the country would have benefited from similar increases in speed, and patterns of development might well have been different. Corridors of similar length to Boston - New York would have experienced similar service wherever population was sufficiently great. Longer distances would not. Eight hour service New York to Chicago, for example, would have held off the DC-3 but would not have successfully met the challenge of two and a quarter-hour jet time. If railroads had been stimulated to exploit their potential for productivity, however, and air service had been required to support its own terminal and control services, the two might well have coexisted at different price levels, giving the customer a real choice. Transcontinental business travel would surely have gone to the air just as it actually did, but it's possible that western railroads might have run some vacation sight-seeing trains.

In freight service portions of the market neglected by the protected railroads would surely have been developed. Less than carload (LCL) service, always important to manufacturers, was treated with contempt by most railroads because it was labor-intensive, absorbed lots of attention, and produced many complaints. There were isolated examples of successful solutions of the various problems involved, but most attempts were half-hearted and stifled by the familiar management attitude that there was nothing to be gained. The New Haven Railroad actually began an experiment with setting up a separate profit center with full decision-making power for the handling of LCL, an unheard-of departure from tradition, and it was beginning to work, but the death of the executive who had the vision and wisdom to try it and the return of more traditional management spelled its doom. If this and the few other successful operations had been uninhibited, however, and other improvement ideas pursued, a truly good LCL service would have been developed. If this had been combined with rate freedom it would have been a great boon to manufacturers, who would not have been so easily persuaded to turn to highway transport. There is no technological reason why highway transport can provide better LCL service at less cost than rail where there is volume. The appearance of better truck service, now for some time accepted as received wisdom, is entirely due to institutional factors, *viz.*: (1) the rigidity of the railroad rate structure, (2) the lack of entrepreneurship in rail management, (3) the intransigeance of rail labor, and (4) government largesse lavished on highways. Without these factors we would have seen automated freight houses, well coordinated delivery service, faster trains, and rates adjusted to market conditions. Trucks would have extended the service to areas where volume could not support rail service. Highways would have cost less to build and maintain and been far pleasanter to drive on without heavy concentrations of truck traffic in those areas where volume could justify rail service.

Branch lines would remain where there was need for them and would not have been artificially preserved where not needed. In the partial deregulation of the 1980s many new small railroads are being formed to operate branch lines which the large roads are finally permitted to shed. Many of these new short lines are supported by taxpayers' money, but not all. It seems highly probable that in a climate of freedom many such lines would have appeared in response to the ability of a small local management to adapt to specific demands with more satisfactory action than that of a relatively clumsy large road. At the same time mergers would presumably have proceeded unhampered to produce truly nationwide railroads, probably two systems each of which served all major cities and other traffic-producing areas. Before regulation in the nineteenth century there were many more mergers than recently. Tiny roads built almost everywhere in the first flush of enthusiasm were rapidly brought together to form the major systems of the turn of the century. The same market forces would presumably have continued until the nation was covered.

Some have suggested that the result would have been a single entity, like AT&T. This seems doubtful simply because no such monopoly has ever existed for so long without government support. The desire to compete for lucrative traffic would be sufficient to bring in a competitor if freedom reigned. That the balance between such competitive urge and the advantages of carrying traffic all the way from origin to destination on one carrier would result in two ubiquitous systems can be supported by an examination of the actual railroad map. Existing lines can be arranged into two systems which serve all points. It has happened in the South; it is probably happening in the East; and it is at least conceptual in the West. It is not possible, however, to produce a third such system without substantial new construction in spite of the over-building of the original enthusiasm. More than one but less than three equals two.

The picture which emerges is of two nation-wide systems, not unlike the Canadian Pacific and Canadian National in our northern neighbor, each serving all major points. Hundreds of short lines might serve lesser traffic points by feeding each of the majors. Motor carriers would have developed into the area of their natural advantage rather than being artificially stimulated into areas where they are neither energy- nor manpower-efficient. Waterways would have thrived where they naturally exist but not have been artificially cut through natural obstacles at great cost to the economy and the environment. Common ownership of various modes, for example, railroad ownership of trucking lines, is problematical. On the one hand it would be natural for a railroad to develop an air line or motor carrier (both passenger and freight) as a means of serving more efficiently the far reaches of its area where light traffic made rail unit costs high. On the other hand roads might well have sensed that they lacked the management know-how to develop a new enterprise better left to enthusiastic specialists. In a free environment there would be some of each unless one arrangement or the other has a strong natural advantage.

One form of intermodal cooperation which would surely have developed earlier and to a much greater degree than it did is the movement of highway trailers or containers on flat cars, called TOFC/COFC, or more picturesquely, piggyback. This is a natural and appealing marriage of methods with complementary skills long ago conceptualized and often tried but beset with even more ritualistic and institutional burdens than railroading itself. Before the advent of the motor truck wagons with and without horses were moved in England and America, but without a motor the scope of the highway vehicle is insufficiently advantageous to support the practice. In the 1930s, however, the New Haven Railroad offered a Boston - New York overnight service with a choice of two schedules, late afternoon departure with arrival just after midnight or evening departure with early morning arrival. The service enjoyed a fairly brisk patronage, but it failed to penetrate the very large market to the extent of more than one or two percent. It was offered for the most part to motor carriers, who found it very convenient for overflow business. They were forbidden by their unions, however, from using it for regular business and were compelled to make a payment to union funds whenever they did use it. That such union power is strengthened by motor carrier regulation has finally become evident now that deregulation has brought modification of union demands.

At the same time, however, the railroad was at a loss to attack the problem. Some 30-40 years later railroads began hesitantly to offer piggyback in a variety of services which covered all variations from road haul alone to full door-to-door service. Even then, however, institutional habits of thought severely restricted what should have been dramatic growth. For one thing, railroad people worried that all the freight carried by piggyback was merely robbing box car traffic, another example of the "we already have all the business" syndrome. For another, every rate innovation was stifled by the worry that another road would demand its suspension by regulatory authority. For another, the preoccupation with certain statistics, such as gross ton-miles per train-mile, inhibited the operation of short, fast trains unencumbered with other traffic. For another, lack of good cost analysis obscured the possibilities of improved equipment utilization by high frequency and fast turns. The insistence of Labor on retention of redundant crewmen and restriction of their actions added to the obstructions.

Just as partial deregulation in the 1980s is slowly correcting these ills, so we might properly assume that a climate of freedom would have produced a far more diverse and rapidly growing coordination. Probably by the 1920s high-speed container trains would have offered service to the vehicles of motor carriers, shippers, or the railroad itself providing door-to-door service. In areas of high volume a frequency of service approaching hourly trains, tailored to fit the hours of least passenger demand, would have ensured full utilization of plant while meeting the challenge of the motor truck's ability to depart at the shipper's convenience. Innovative rate changes would have related prices to cost and to demand in such a way as to even out traffic flow and maximize efficiency. The development of the motor truck would have brought the advantages of this superior transport service to areas not served by rail or inefficiently served by low-volume branch lines. In other words the development of the motor truck would not have been thwarted but rather directed to the area of its natural advantage and greatest contribution.

Probably the most felicitous change which might reasonably have been expected is in labor relations. The combination of quasi-monopoly and growth inhibition which resulted from regulation produced the worst possible atmosphere for progressive conditions of employment. Any indication that technological change might render a position redundant led to confrontation which usually ended in arbitrary freezing of jobs and practices. This induced a similar stubbornness on management's part in clinging to any apparent advantage traditionally held. This impasse can be broken only if (1) vigorous growth so nurtures increase in demand for labor as to make it obvious that stubborn clinging to outdated methods is counterproductive, (2) the same increase in demand strengthens Labor's bargaining position, and (3) freedom of competition assures the expression of the wishes of individual workers. In short, the growth which freedom would have induced would have assured high wages, short hours, and probably participation in decision making without the necessity of retaining redundant positions and practices.

Probably the most tragic effect of the impasse in labor relations brought about by the stunting of growth is the ruthless killing off of the opportunities for automation which are inherent in railroad technology. Because the flanged wheels of railroad vehicles are guided by the rails and because the rails provide conduits for electric currents which can be used for control, the automation of operation on rails is much easier than the automation of any other form of transport except elevators. The development of this potential has been restricted to one or two small private installations carrying coal from mine to generating plant, but even these tiny applications prove that the concept is perfectly practicable. It is, of course, thwarted in general because Labor has the same natural human fear of loss of jobs which inspired the Luddites. This can only be overcome by the growth which provides guarantee of absorption of displaced labor. The telephone companies, for example, automated their operations without, it is said, laying off anyone. The resultant sharp reduction in costs and rates over the years has been a boon and an inspiration. Similar effect on railroad rates and charges would have brought them well below any alternative, adding still more to the growth spiral.

In the late 1950s John W. Barriger, a railroad executive of unusual vision and wide acquaintance, wrote *Super Railroads*. The burden of his argument was that rail technology needed volume and growth to reach its potential and that growth had been denied by the effects of regulation. He called for the same kind of drastic improvement in alignment and track which was beginning to be incorporated in superhighways. He visualized 100 mile-per-hour passenger service and 70 mile-per-hour freight, considered visionary by many, but more modest than we have suggested would have occurred a generation earlier if freedom had prevailed. His thesis is fundamentally the same as ours, that freedom would have permitted innovation, growth followed by cost reduction leading to further growth, all of which would have developed the potential of the basic technology far beyond what has in fact occurred. There is a story, probably apocryphal, that when Eisenhower's administration was planning the inter-state highway system it was suggested that a similar network of superrailroads be included. The story is that the railroads refused to consider becoming involved with a government scheme. Whether true or not this report is certainly consist-ent with the attitude of most railroad managers toward government operation, always considered anathema. Furthermore, it's probably just as well, since the construction would have been directed by political log-rolling rather than by need and prospects. It would also probably have increased the governmental control which has caused most of the trouble.

In other countries railroad development has been curiously spotty. European and Japanese railways have never developed their freight-carrying abilities or markets even to the extent accomplished here. The reason apparently has to do with the much older and more intensive development of waterways, both natural and artificial, whose traditions led to enough favorable treatment to prevent the railways from exploiting heavy freight service. On the other hand passenger service developed quickly because of heavy population concentrations in relatively close proximity. Because automobiles and gasoline were taxed heavily the use of autos for intercity travel did not develop so fast as here. Intensive development of high-speed potential has recently been pursued, and the resulting excellent service is always a marvel to American tourists. The result is a curious inversion of our situation. Lack of heavy freight development and enormous labor redundancy for political reasons has led to tremendous deficits, while passenger service has risen to creditable heights. In Japan, for example, the rail deficit is an embarrassment to the government, amounting to a substantial portion of the total government deficit. On the other hand, the superb Shin Kansen, the high-speed service so widely publicized, carries more passengers in a day than Amtrak carries in a year on a comparable route and makes so much money that it paid off its very high cost of construction in a decade.

In short, if development had been uninhibited we should by now have a railroad system making great contribution to our economy and our life style. Passenger train speeds of 150 miles per hour would be commonplace in those areas where volume made it feasible and distance was not so great as to make jet speed's advantage compelling. Freight trains for high-value merchandise would be almost as fast. The prices of both would be much lower, leading to the possible extension of high-speed passenger services over greater distances at fares lower than air. Highways would be cheaper to build and pleasanter to drive on. Possibly, if deregulation continues and response is uninhibited, some of this may yet come about, but it's late, and about a century has been lost.